The Complete
30-Day
Whole Food

Cookbook for Beginners

Simple and Nutritious 30-Day Whole Food Recipes to Transform
Your Eating Habits and Bring You a Whole New Lifestyle

Judith Dimaggio

CONTENTS

Introduction

The 30-Day Whole Foods Diet is not just a diet; it's a lifestyle change that encourages you to consume foods in their most natural, unprocessed form. This diet is designed to reset your body, helping you break free from unhealthy eating habits, regain your energy, and discover a healthier version of yourself. By committing to this 30-day journey, you'll focus on eating whole, nutrient-dense foods that nourish your body, while avoiding processed foods, added sugars, and artificial ingredients. The goal is to transform your relationship with food and set the foundation for lifelong healthy eating habits.

At its core, the Whole Foods Diet emphasizes eating foods that are as close to their natural state as possible. This means choosing foods that are minimally processed, free from artificial additives, and packed with nutrients. The philosophy is simple: the less a food is altered from its original form, the more it retains its nutritional value. Whole foods include fresh fruits and vegetables, lean proteins, nuts, seeds, and healthy fats. These foods are rich in vitamins, minerals, and antioxidants that support overall health and well-being.

Embarking on a 30-day Whole Foods Diet can bring about a myriad of health benefits. One of the most significant advantages is improved digestion. Processed foods are often loaded with additives and preservatives that can disrupt the digestive system. By eliminating these foods and focusing on whole foods, you may experience better digestion, reduced bloating, and improved gut health.

Another key benefit is enhanced energy levels. Many people report feeling more energized and alert when they switch to a whole foods diet. This is because whole foods provide a steady source of energy, unlike processed foods that can cause blood sugar spikes and crashes. By fueling your body with nutrient-dense foods, you'll likely notice a sustained increase in energy throughout the day.

The 30-Day Whole Foods Diet can also contribute to weight loss. Whole foods are generally lower in calories and higher in fiber, which helps you feel full and satisfied. Additionally, by cutting out processed foods and added sugars, you're likely to reduce your overall calorie intake without feeling deprived. This natural approach to weight loss is sustainable and can lead to long-term success.

The 30-Day Whole Foods Diet is a powerful tool for transforming your health and resetting your relationship with food. By focusing on whole, nutrient-dense foods, you can experience a range of benefits, from improved digestion and increased energy to sustainable weight loss. This 30-day journey is an opportunity to nourish your body, develop healthier eating habits, and lay the foundation for a lifetime of wellness. Embrace the challenge, and discover the positive changes that come from eating whole foods.

Fundamentals of 30-Day Whole Foods

The 30-Day Whole Foods diet focuses on eating unprocessed, natural foods to reset and improve your eating habits. It emphasizes consuming whole, nutrient-dense ingredients like fruits, vegetables, and lean proteins while eliminating processed foods, added sugars, and artificial additives. This diet encourages a back-to-basics approach to nutrition, promoting a healthier lifestyle by nourishing the body with wholesome, real foods. By following this plan, individuals aim to boost their energy levels, improve digestion, and support overall well-being within a 30-day period.

What Is 30-Day Whole Foods?

The 30-Day Whole Foods Diet is a nutrition plan that emphasizes consuming only natural, unprocessed foods for 30 days to help reset your body, improve overall health, and develop sustainable eating habits. This diet eliminates all processed foods, added sugars, refined grains, dairy, alcohol, and artificial ingredients, focusing instead on nutrient-dense whole foods like fruits, vegetables, lean proteins, nuts, seeds, and healthy fats. It is designed to cleanse your system, promote weight loss, enhance digestion, and boost energy levels.

The primary goal of the 30-Day Whole Foods Diet is to reset

your body's natural rhythm by eliminating foods that can cause inflammation, digestive issues, and energy fluctuations. The idea is that by removing these potentially harmful foods and replacing them with nutrient-rich alternatives, your body can better regulate itself, resulting in improved physical and mental health.

The 30-Day Whole Foods diet is more than just a temporary eating plan; it's a transformative journey toward a healthier, more mindful way of living. Over the course of 30 days, this diet encourages you to embrace the simplicity and nourishment that comes from consuming natural, unprocessed foods. By focusing on whole foods—such as vegetables, fruits, lean proteins, nuts, and seeds— you're giving your body the nutrients it needs to function at its best. Throughout this journey, you've likely experienced a variety of benefits, from increased energy and improved digestion to better skin and weight management. These changes are a testament to the power of whole foods and their ability to support overall health and well-being. The 30-Day Whole Foods diet not only helps reset your eating habits but also teaches you the importance of choosing foods that are closest to their natural state.

One of the key takeaways from this diet is the understanding that food is fuel for your body, and the quality of that fuel matters. By eliminating processed foods, added sugars, and artificial ingredients, you've allowed your body to detoxify and function more efficiently. The focus on nutrient-dense foods means you're not just eating to fill your stomach but to nourish your body from the inside out.

Sticking to the 30-Day Whole Foods diet may have had its challenges, especially in the beginning. However, as you progressed, you likely found that the diet became easier to

follow, particularly as you discovered new recipes, meal-planning strategies, and healthy substitutes for your favorite processed foods. This journey has undoubtedly strengthened your willpower and discipline, qualities that will serve you well beyond these 30 days.

The diet's emphasis on planning and preparation has also likely instilled in you a greater appreciation for home-cooked meals. By taking control of your food choices and meal preparation, you've minimized reliance on convenience foods and fast food, which often lack nutritional value. Instead, you've prioritized foods that are fresh, wholesome, and prepared with care.

As you conclude the 30-Day Whole Foods diet, it's important to reflect on what you've learned and how you can carry these lessons forward. This diet isn't meant to be a restrictive or temporary fix; rather, it's a foundation upon which you can build a lifelong commitment to healthy eating. Whether you choose to continue with a strict whole foods approach or incorporate some flexibility into your diet, the principles you've learned will continue to guide your food choices.

Moreover, the positive changes you've experienced—whether physical, mental, or emotional—are a powerful reminder of the impact that food has on your overall health. The increased energy, improved mood, and enhanced well-being are all testaments to the fact that what you eat truly matters.

What to Eat on the 30-Day Whole Foods Diet

The 30-Day Whole Foods Diet emphasizes consuming unprocessed, natural, and nutrient-dense foods. The goal is to focus on real ingredients that provide essential vitamins, minerals, and nutrients, supporting overall health and well-being. Here's a detailed look at what to eat on this diet:

1.Fruits and Vegetables

Why Eat Them: Fruits and vegetables are rich in vitamins, minerals, fiber, and antioxidants. They support digestive health, boost the immune system, and reduce the risk of chronic diseases.

Examples:

Fruits: Apples, bananas, berries, oranges, grapes, melons, and avocados.

Vegetables: Leafy greens (spinach, kale, arugula), cruciferous vegetables (broccoli, cauliflower, Brussels sprouts), root vegetables (sweet potatoes, carrots, beets), and others like peppers, cucumbers, and zucchini.

Tips: Aim to include a variety of colors and types in your diet to ensure a broad spectrum of nutrients.

2.Lean Proteins

Why Eat Them: Proteins are the building blocks of the body, crucial for muscle repair, enzyme production, and overall cellular function.

Examples:

Animal Proteins: Grass-fed beef, free-range chicken, turkey, lamb, and wild-caught fish like salmon, mackerel, and sardines.

Plant-Based Proteins: Legumes (lentils, chickpeas, black beans), tofu, tempeh, and edamame.

Tips: Opt for organic, free-range, or wild-caught options when possible to avoid added hormones and antibiotics.

3.Healthy Fats

Why Eat Them: Healthy fats are essential for brain function, hormone production, and absorbing fat-soluble vitamins (A, D, E, K).

Examples:

Plant-Based Fats: Avocado, nuts (almonds, walnuts, cashews), seeds (chia seeds, flaxseeds, pumpkin seeds), and olives.

Oils: Extra virgin olive oil, coconut oil, and avocado oil.

Tips: Use these fats in moderation and avoid hydrogenated oils and trans fats commonly found in processed foods.

4.Nuts and Seeds

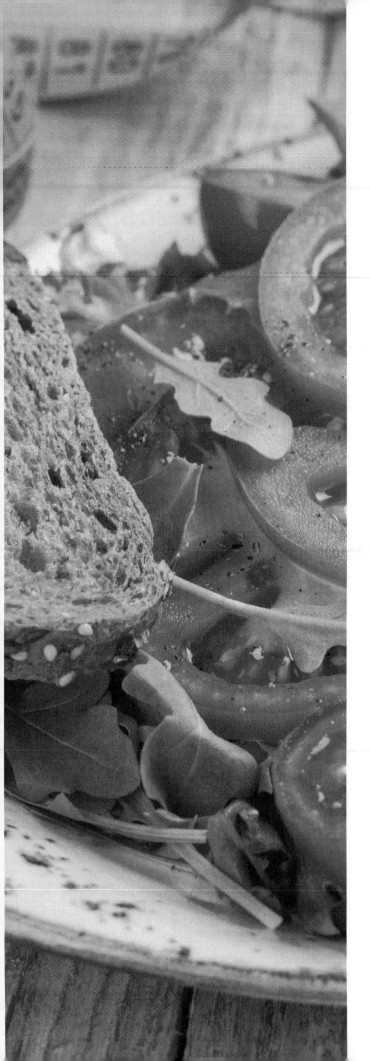

Why Eat Them: Nuts and seeds are rich in healthy fats, protein, fiber, and a variety of vitamins and minerals, making them excellent for heart health and energy.

Examples:

Almonds, walnuts, flaxseeds, chia seeds, sunflower seeds, and hemp seeds.

Tips: Choose raw or dry-roasted nuts without added oils or sugars. They make a great snack or topping for salads and smoothies.

5.Legumes

Why Eat Them: Legumes are packed with protein, fiber, and essential nutrients like iron and folate. They are also low in fat and high in complex carbohydrates.

Examples:

Lentils, black beans, chickpeas, kidney beans, and peas.

Tips: If you're sensitive to legumes, start with smaller portions and gradually increase your intake to allow your digestive system to adjust.

6.Herbs and Spices

Why Eat Them: Herbs and spices add flavor without added calories, sugars, or unhealthy fats. They also provide antioxidants and have anti-inflammatory properties.

Examples:

Fresh herbs (basil, parsley, cilantro, mint) and spices (turmeric, cinnamon, ginger, garlic, and cumin).

Tips: Experiment with a variety of herbs and spices to enhance the flavor of your dishes naturally.

7.Beverages

Why Drink Them: Hydration is essential for overall health, aiding in digestion, nutrient transport, and temperature regulation.

Examples:

Water, herbal teas, and black coffee (without added sugar or creamers).

Tips: Avoid sugary drinks and limit alcohol. Aim for at least eight glasses of water a day.

What to Avoid on the 30-Day Whole Foods Diet

The 30-Day Whole Foods Diet emphasizes eliminating processed and refined foods that offer little nutritional value and may contribute to health issues like obesity, diabetes, and heart disease. Here's what to avoid:

1.Processed Foods

Why Avoid Them: Processed foods are often high in unhealthy fats, sugars, and sodium while being low in essential nutrients. They can contribute to weight gain, inflammation, and chronic diseases.

Examples:

Packaged snacks (chips, cookies, crackers), fast food, frozen meals, and instant noodles.

Tips: Stick to whole, unprocessed foods that don't come in a box or a bag. Always check the ingredient list for added preservatives, artificial flavors, and chemicals.

2.Refined Grains

Why Avoid Them: Refined grains are stripped of their fiber, vitamins, and minerals, leading to rapid spikes in blood sugar levels and providing empty calories.

Examples:

White bread, white rice, pasta made from refined flour, and breakfast cereals.

Tips: Replace refined grains with whole grains like quinoa, brown rice, and whole oats to maintain stable energy levels. And of course, it's best to skip grains as much as possible.

3.Added Sugars

Why Avoid Them: Excessive sugar intake can lead to weight gain, insulin resistance, and an increased risk of type 2 diabetes and heart disease.

Examples:

Sugary drinks (sodas, sweetened teas), desserts (cakes, pastries, candies), and processed foods with added sugars (ketchup, salad dressings, and sauces).

Tips: Be mindful of hidden sugars in foods like sauces, dressings, and packaged snacks. Opt for natural sweeteners like honey or maple syrup in moderation if needed.

4.Artificial Sweeteners

Why Avoid Them: Artificial sweeteners may disrupt gut health and contribute to sugar cravings and metabolic disorders.

Examples:

Aspartame, sucralose, saccharin, and acesulfame potassium (found in diet sodas, sugar-free gum, and low-calorie desserts).

Tips: Instead of artificial sweeteners, use natural alternatives like stevia or monk fruit in moderation.

5.Unhealthy Fats

Why Avoid Them: Trans fats and unhealthy saturated fats can raise LDL (bad) cholesterol levels, increasing the risk of heart disease.

Examples:

Margarine, shortening, hydrogenated oils, fried foods, and commercially baked goods.

Tips: Choose healthy fats from avocados, nuts, seeds, and olive oil, and avoid products labeled as containing "partially hydrogenated oils."

6.Dairy Products

Why Avoid Them: Some individuals find that dairy can cause inflammation, digestive issues, and contribute to skin problems like acne.

Examples:

Milk, cheese, yogurt, butter, and cream.

Tips: Consider dairy alternatives like almond milk, coconut yogurt, and cashew cheese if you are sensitive to dairy. If you consume dairy, choose organic, grass-fed options.

7.Alcohol

Why Avoid It: Alcohol can be high in empty calories, lead to poor food choices, disrupt sleep, and affect liver function.

Examples:

Beer, wine, spirits, and cocktails.

Tips: If you choose to drink, do so in moderation. Opt for low-sugar options like dry wine or spirits mixed with soda water, but be mindful that alcohol can still hinder your progress.

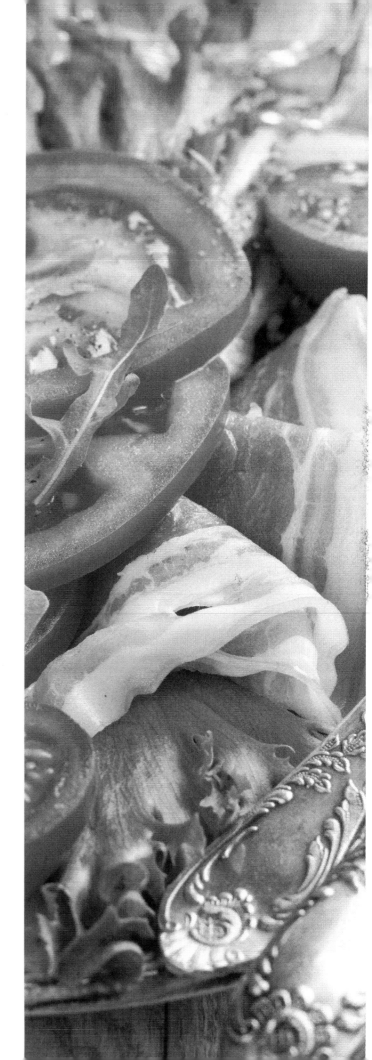

8.Processed Meats

Why Avoid Them: Processed meats are often high in sodium, nitrates, and preservatives, which can increase the risk of cancer, heart disease, and other health issues.

Examples:

Bacon, sausages, hot dogs, deli meats, and canned meats.

Tips: Focus on fresh, lean meats and fish. If you eat cured meats, look for those that are nitrate-free and minimally processed.

9.Artificial Additives and Preservatives

Why Avoid Them: Artificial additives and preservatives can cause allergic reactions, digestive issues, and disrupt the body's natural processes.

Examples:

Monosodium glutamate (MSG), artificial food colorings, and preservatives like BHT and BHA.

Tips: Read labels carefully and avoid products with long ingredient lists full of unrecognizable chemicals. Stick to fresh, whole foods whenever possible.

10.Gluten (for those sensitive)

Why Avoid It: Some individuals may experience digestive discomfort, bloating, and inflammation when consuming gluten.

Examples:

Wheat, barley, rye, and products containing them like bread, pasta, and beer.

Tips: Opt for gluten-free grains like quinoa, rice, and gluten-free oats.

The 30-Day Whole Foods Diet encourages a return to natural, unprocessed foods that provide the body with essential nutrients. By focusing on whole fruits and vegetables, lean proteins, and healthy fats, this diet supports overall health and well-being. At the same time, it eliminates foods that are processed, high in sugar, or contain unhealthy fats and additives, which can contribute to various health issues. Following this plan for 30 days can lead to better energy levels, improved digestion, and a stronger foundation for long-term healthy eating habits.

Benefits of 30-Day Whole Foods

The 30-Day Whole Foods Diet is designed to help individuals reset their eating habits by focusing on whole, unprocessed foods. This diet offers numerous advantages that contribute to overall health, well-being, and long-term sustainable lifestyle changes. Below, I've outlined the key benefits of the 30-Day Whole Foods Diet, divided into various categories to provide a comprehensive understanding of its impact.

Promotes Nutrient-Dense Eating

The cornerstone of the 30-Day Whole Foods Diet is the emphasis on nutrient dense foods. By eliminating processed foods, which are often high in empty calories and low in essential nutrients, this diet encourages the consumption of foods rich in vitamins, minerals, and antioxidants. Whole foods like fruits, vegetables, lean proteins, nuts, and seeds are packed with the nutrients your body needs to function optimally. This nutrient-dense approach not only supports physical health but also enhances energy levels, cognitive function, and overall vitality.

Supports Healthy Weight Loss

One of the primary reasons people choose the 30-Day Whole Foods Diet is its effectiveness in promoting healthy weight loss. By focusing on whole, unprocessed foods and eliminating added sugars, refined grains, and unhealthy fats, this diet naturally reduces caloric intake without the need for calorie counting. The high fiber content of whole foods helps you feel fuller for longer, reducing the likelihood of overeating. Additionally, by avoiding processed foods, which often contain hidden sugars and unhealthy fats, you can more easily achieve and maintain a healthy weight.

Improves Digestive Health

The 30-Day Whole Foods Diet is particularly beneficial for digestive health. Processed foods are often laden with artificial additives, preservatives, and unhealthy fats that can irritate the digestive system and cause issues like bloating, gas, and constipation. In contrast, whole foods are rich in fiber, which promotes regular bowel movements, supports gut health, and helps prevent digestive disorders. By consuming a diet high in fruits, vegetables, and legumes, you can improve your digestion and reduce the risk of gastrointestinal problems.

Reduces Inflammation

Chronic inflammation is a key contributor to many health problems, including heart disease, diabetes, and autoimmune disorders. The 30-Day Whole Foods Diet helps reduce inflammation by eliminating foods that are known to trigger inflammatory

responses, such as refined sugars, processed meats, and unhealthy fats. Instead, the diet emphasizes anti-inflammatory foods like leafy greens, fatty fish, nuts, and seeds, which are rich in omega-3 fatty acids and antioxidants. By following this diet, you can reduce inflammation in the body, leading to improved overall health and a lower risk of chronic diseases.

Enhances Mental Clarity and Focus

The foods you eat have a significant impact on your mental clarity and cognitive function. Processed foods, particularly those high in sugar and unhealthy fats, can lead to brain fog, decreased focus, and impaired memory. The 30-Day Whole Foods Diet supports brain health by providing the nutrients needed for optimal cognitive function, such as omega-3 fatty acids, antioxidants, and B vitamins. By following this diet, you may experience improved mental clarity, better focus, and enhanced memory, all of which contribute to a higher quality of life.

Balances Blood Sugar Levels

Maintaining stable blood sugar levels is crucial for overall health, particularly for individuals with diabetes or those at risk of developing the condition. The 30-Day Whole Foods Diet helps regulate blood sugar levels by eliminating refined sugars and processed carbohydrates, which can cause spikes and crashes in blood glucose. Instead, the diet focuses on lean proteins and healthy fats, which provide a steady release of energy and help prevent blood sugar fluctuations. This balanced approach to eating can reduce the risk of insulin resistance and type 2 diabetes.

Boosts Energy Levels

Many people who follow the 30-Day Whole Foods Diet report a significant increase in energy levels. Processed foods can drain your energy by causing blood sugar spikes and crashes, leading to fatigue and sluggishness. In contrast, whole foods provide a steady source of energy throughout the day, thanks to their balanced macronutrient content and high fiber levels. By fueling your body with nutrient-dense foods, you can maintain consistent energy levels, improve your stamina, and feel more energized and productive.

Supports Heart Health

Heart disease is one of the leading causes of death worldwide, but the 30-Day Whole Foods Diet can help reduce your risk. This diet emphasizes foods that are known to support heart health, such as fruits, vegetables, nuts, seeds, and lean proteins. These foods are rich in heart-healthy nutrients like fiber, potassium, magnesium, and omega-3 fatty acids, which help lower cholesterol levels, reduce blood pressure, and improve overall cardiovascular function. By following this diet, you can take proactive steps to protect your heart and reduce your risk of heart disease.

Encourages Mindful Eating

One of the less obvious but equally important benefits of the 30-Day Whole Foods Diet is that it encourages mindful eating. In our fast-paced world, it's easy to fall into the habit of mindlessly consuming processed foods without paying attention to hunger cues or the nutritional value of what we're eating. This diet requires you to be more intentional about your food choices, which can help you develop a healthier relationship with food. By practicing mindful eating, you can better recognize when you're truly hungry, enjoy your meals more, and avoid overeating.

Fosters Long-Term Healthy Habits

The 30-Day Whole Foods Diet is not just a temporary diet; it's a powerful tool for fostering long-term healthy habits. By committing to this diet for 30 days, you can reset your palate, break unhealthy eating patterns, and develop a taste for whole, natural foods. Many people find that after completing the 30 days, they continue to incorporate whole foods into their diet and make healthier choices

overall. This diet serves as a foundation for a lifetime of healthy eating, helping you maintain your weight, improve your health, and feel your best for years to come.

In summary, the 30-Day Whole Foods Diet offers a multitude of benefits that go beyond just weight loss. By focusing on whole, unprocessed foods, this diet can improve your digestion, reduce inflammation, enhance mental clarity, balance blood sugar levels, and support heart health. Additionally, it encourages mindful eating and fosters long-term healthy habits, making it an excellent choice for anyone looking to reset their diet and improve their overall well-being. Whether you're looking to lose weight, increase your energy levels, or simply eat healthier, the 30-Day Whole Foods Diet provides a comprehensive and sustainable approach to achieving your health goals.

How to Stick with 30-Day Whole Foods

Sticking to the 30-Day Whole Foods diet can be a transformative experience, but it requires planning, discipline, and motivation. Here's a comprehensive guide on how to successfully navigate and adhere to this diet plan:

Understand the Basics of the Whole Foods Diet

Before embarking on the 30-Day Whole Foods journey, it's crucial to understand what the diet entails. This diet focuses on consuming unprocessed, natural foods such as vegetables, fruits, lean proteins, nuts, and seeds. Processed foods, refined sugars, and artificial ingredients are strictly avoided. Knowing these fundamentals will help you make informed choices and stay committed.

Set Clear Goals

Having a clear reason for starting the 30-Day Whole Foods diet can help you stay focused. Whether your goal is weight loss, improving your energy levels, or adopting a healthier lifestyle, write it down and remind yourself of it daily. Setting both short-term and long-term goals will give you something to strive for and keep you motivated throughout the process.

Plan Your Meals in Advance

Meal planning is a critical aspect of sticking to the 30-Day Whole Foods diet. Take time each week to plan your meals, ensuring that each one aligns with the diet's principles. Planning helps prevent impulsive decisions that could lead to unhealthy choices. Create a shopping list based on your meal plan, and make sure your kitchen is stocked with whole, unprocessed foods.

Prepare Your Meals Ahead of Time

Meal prepping can save time and reduce the temptation to reach for convenient, processed options. Dedicate a day each week to prepare meals in bulk, such as cooking large batches of grains, roasting vegetables, and pre-cooking proteins. Store these in portioned containers so you have healthy meals ready to go throughout the week.

Keep Healthy Snacks On Hand

Cravings can be a challenge, especially when starting a new diet. Combat this by keeping healthy, whole food snacks available. Nuts, seeds, fruit, and vegetable sticks are great options. Having these snacks readily available will help you resist the urge to reach for processed foods when hunger strikes.

Stay Hydrated

Drinking plenty of water is essential on the 30-Day Whole Foods diet. Often, our bodies confuse thirst with hunger, leading to unnecessary snacking. Make it a habit to drink water throughout the day, especially

fore meals. Herbal teas and infused water are also good options to stay drated while adding variety to your fluid intake.

ducate Yourself on Whole Foods

nowledge is power, and understanding the benefits of whole ods can reinforce your commitment to the diet. Learn about the tritional value of different foods, how they affect your body, and hy processed foods are detrimental to your health. This knowledge ill not only keep you motivated but also help you make better food oices.

ind Healthy Substitutes

ne of the keys to sticking with the 30-Day Whole Foods diet is nding healthy substitutes for your favorite processed foods. For ample, if you crave something sweet, choose fruits or homemade acks made with natural sweeteners like dates or honey. Substituting ealthier options will satisfy your cravings without breaking the diet.

ractice Mindful Eating

indful eating involves paying full attention to the eating experience, voring each bite, and recognizing hunger and fullness cues. This actice can help you develop a healthier relationship with food and void overeating. Focus on the flavors, textures, and satisfaction ou get from eating whole foods. Mindful eating can also help you ppreciate the benefits of the diet and stay on track.

void Temptations

uring the 30-day period, try to avoid situations where you may e tempted to eat processed or unhealthy foods. This could mean declining invitations to restaurants that don't offer healthy options or bringing your own meal to social gatherings. Surround yourself with like-minded individuals who support your dietary goals, and minimize exposure to environments that may lead to temptation.

Join a Support Group

Joining a support group, either online or in person, can provide motivation and encouragement. Sharing your experiences, challenges, and successes with others who are also following the 30-Day Whole Foods diet can keep you accountable. Support groups can also be a great source of new recipes, meal ideas, and tips for staying on track.

Stay Positive and Be Patient

Adopting a new diet can be challenging, and there may be moments of frustration or temptation. It's important to stay positive and remind yourself that you're making a long-term investment in your health. Don't be too hard on yourself if you slip up; instead, refocus and get back on track as soon as possible. Progress is more important than perfection.

Track Your Progress

Keeping a journal of your meals, mood, energy levels, and physical changes can be a powerful tool for staying committed. Tracking your progress helps you see the benefits of the diet, such as weight loss, improved digestion, and increased energy. Celebrate your successes, no matter how small, and use them as motivation to continue.

Experiment with New Recipes

Variety is the spice of life, and trying new recipes can keep your meals exciting and prevent boredom. Experiment with different whole foods, spices, and cooking methods to discover new favorite dishes. The more you enjoy your meals, the easier it will be to stick with the diet.

Incorporate Exercise

Regular physical activity complements the 30-Day Whole Foods diet by enhancing your overall health and well-being. Exercise helps regulate blood sugar, boosts metabolism, and supports weight management. Find an exercise routine that you enjoy, whether it's walking, yoga, or weight training, and make it a part of your daily routine.

Listen to Your Body

Everyone's body responds differently to dietary changes. Pay attention to how your body feels throughout the 30 days. If you notice positive changes, such as increased energy or better digestion, use these as motivators to keep going. If you experience any negative symptoms, adjust your diet accordingly and consult a healthcare professional if needed.

Prepare for Post-Diet Transition

As the 30-day period comes to an end, plan how you'll transition back to a more flexible eating plan while maintaining the principles of whole foods. Consider incorporating some of your favorite recipes from the diet into your regular meal rotation. The goal is to make whole foods a permanent part of your lifestyle, even after the 30 days are over.

Reflect on Your Experience

At the end of the 30 days, take time to reflect on your experience. Consider what you've learned, how you feel, and what changes you've noticed in your health and well-being. Use these reflections to set new goals and continue your journey toward a healthier lifestyle.

Celebrate Your Success

Completing the 30-Day Whole Foods diet is an accomplishment worth celebrating. Reward yourself with a non-food-related treat, such as a massage, a new workout outfit, or a day trip. Recognizing your success reinforces positive behavior and sets the stage for continued healthy habits.

Make Whole Foods a Lifestyle

Ultimately, the 30-Day Whole Foods diet is not just a short-term challenge but a step toward a healthier lifestyle. Use the habits and knowledge you've gained during these 30 days to make whole foods a permanent part of your diet. By doing so, you'll continue to reap the benefits of a nutritious, balanced diet for years to come.

By following these tips and staying committed, you can successfully navigate the 30-Day Whole Foods diet and set the foundation for a healthier, more vibrant life.

4-Week Meal Plan

Week 1

Day 1:
Breakfast: Shakshuka
Lunch: Roasted Tempeh and Vegetable Power Bowl
Snack: No-Bake Nutty Date Bars
Dinner: Garlicky Rosemary Chicken Thighs

Day 2:
Breakfast: Sweet Potato Breakfast Hash with Eggs and Vegetables
Lunch: Vegetable Kebabs
Snack: Sautéed Zucchini with Cherry Tomatoes
Dinner: Seared Sea Scallops with Spring Vegetables

Day 3:
Breakfast: Homemade Marinara Eggs with Parsley
Lunch: Baked Sweet Potato, Chickpea, and Zucchini
Snack: Roasted Broccoli and Cauliflower with Turkey Bacon
Dinner: Flank Steak with Artichokes

Day 4:
Breakfast: California Breakfast Egg White Scramble
Lunch: Healthy Cannellini Bean Lettuce Wraps
Snack: Italian Roasted Vegetables
Dinner: Lemony Chicken Kebabs

Day 5:
Breakfast: Kale Pomegranate Smoothie
Lunch: Israeli Eggplant with Chickpea and Mint
Snack: Lemon Roasted Asparagus
Dinner: Crushed Marcona Almond Swordfish

Day 6:
Breakfast: Asparagus and Cherry Tomato Omelets
Lunch: Roasted Cauliflower Steaks with Eggplant Relish
Snack: Garlic-Lemon Hummus
Dinner: Grilled Steak, Mushroom, and Onion Kebabs

Day 7:
Breakfast: Baked Mushroom and Spinach Egg Cups
Lunch: Healthy Greek Roasted Vegetable Bowl
Snack: Trail Mix
Dinner: Lamb and Cauliflower Pilaff

Week 2

Day 1:
Breakfast: Sweet Potato Hash with Mushrooms
Lunch: Sautéed Greens
Snack: Crunchy Turmeric-Spiced Chickpeas
Dinner: Parsley Chicken and Potatoes

Day 2:
Breakfast: Tofu Scramble
Lunch: Split Pea and Tomato Tabbouleh
Snack: Turkish-Spiced Nuts
Dinner: Flavorful Fish Stew

Day 3:
Breakfast: Egg in a "Pepper Hole" with Avocado Salsa
Lunch: Oven Roasted Vegetable Mélange
Snack: Pickled Turnips
Dinner: Spice-Rubbed Pork Tenderloin

Day 4:
Breakfast: Garlicky Brussels Sprout Hash and Eggs
Lunch: Perfect Patatas Bravas
Snack: Crispy Garlic Oven Baked Potatoes
Dinner: Lemon Chicken and Roasted Artichokes

Day 5:
Breakfast: Fried Eggs with Garlic Swiss Chard and Bell Pepper
Lunch: Hearty Ratatouille
Snack: Crunchy Orange Chickpeas
Dinner: Tilapia with Red Onion and Avocado

Day 6:
Breakfast: Turkey Breakfast Sausage Patties
Lunch: Tunisian Eggs with Tomatoes and Peppers
Snack: Boiled Artichokes with Aioli
Dinner: Roasted Steak and Broccoli

Day 7:
Breakfast: Easy Poached Eggs
Lunch: Rosemary Roasted Red Potatoes
Snack: Sautéed Olives with Garlic
Dinner: Lamb and Bean Stew

Week 3

Day 1:
Breakfast: Sweet Potato Hash with Turkey Sausage Patties
Lunch: Simple Roasted Radishes
Snack: Moroccan Zucchini Spread
Dinner: White Beans and Chicken Stew

Day 2:
Breakfast: Sweet Potato Breakfast Hash with Eggs and Vegetables
Lunch: Garlic Zucchini with Red Pepper
Snack: Sautéed Almonds with Apricots
Dinner: Orange-Garlic Shrimp

Day 3:
Breakfast: Homemade Marinara Eggs with Parsley
Lunch: Italian Orange and Celery Salad
Snack: Lemon Shrimp with Garlic Olive Oil Dipping
Dinner: Lebanese Beef Kebabs with Pickled Red Onions

Day 4:
Breakfast: Shakshuka
Lunch: Mexican Cauliflower Rice
Snack: Red Pepper Tapenade
Dinner: Italian Chicken and Sausage Cacciatore

Day 5:
Breakfast: Kale Pomegranate Smoothie
Lunch: Salmon, Citrus, and Avocado Salad
Snack: Garlic Roasted Tomatoes and Olives
Dinner: Simple Bouillabaisse

Day 6:
Breakfast: California Breakfast Egg White Scramble
Lunch: Sautéed Green Beans with Garlic and Ginger
Snack: Taco Fries
Dinner: Sautéed Pork Loin with Pears

Day 7:
Breakfast: Asparagus and Cherry Tomato Omelets
Lunch: Old-Fashioned Sweet Potato Bake with Pecans
Snack: Pickled Red Onions
Dinner: Pork Stew with Leeks

Week 4

Day 1:
Breakfast: Baked Mushroom and Spinach Egg Cups
Lunch: Roasted Tempeh and Vegetable Power Bowl
Snack: No-Bake Nutty Date Bars
Dinner: Chicken and Chickpea Stew

Day 2:
Breakfast: Egg in a "Pepper Hole" with Avocado Salsa
Lunch: Baked Sweet Potato, Chickpea, and Zucchini
Snack: Smoky Deviled Eggs
Dinner: Spicy Shrimp Puttanesca

Day 3:
Breakfast: Sweet Potato Hash with Mushrooms
Lunch: Vegetable Kebabs
Snack: Trail Mix
Dinner: Herbed Pork Cutlets and Roasted Asparagus

Day 4:
Breakfast: Tofu Scramble
Lunch: Healthy Cannellini Bean Lettuce Wraps
Snack: Crunchy Turmeric-Spiced Chickpeas
Dinner: Traditional Chicken Kalamata

Day 5:
Breakfast: Fried Eggs with Garlic Swiss Chard and Bell Pepper
Lunch: Israeli Eggplant with Chickpea and Mint
Snack: Turkish-Spiced Nuts
Dinner: Cod with Fresh Tomato Salsa

Day 6:
Breakfast: Garlicky Brussels Sprout Hash and Eggs
Lunch: Roasted Cauliflower Steaks with Eggplant Relish
Snack: Pickled Turnips
Dinner: Tuscan Steak with Salsa Verde

Day 7:
Breakfast: Sweet Potato Hash with Turkey Sausage Patties
Lunch: Healthy Greek Roasted Vegetable Bowl
Snack: Crunchy Orange Chickpeas
Dinner: Chili-Spiced Lamb Chops

Chapter 1 Breakfast

Sweet Potato Breakfast Hash with Eggs and Vegetables

Prep Time: 10 minutes | Cook Time: 20 minutes | Serves: 4

2 tablespoons extra-virgin olive oil

3 cups peeled and cubed sweet potato (½-inch pieces) (2 to 3 sweet potatoes)

1 cup diced yellow bell pepper

1 cup diced yellow onion

1 teaspoon paprika

¼ teaspoon salt

3 cups chopped kale

2 garlic cloves, minced

4 pasteurized large eggs

⅛ teaspoon freshly ground black pepper

Salsa, for serving (optional)

1. In a large skillet, heat the olive oil over medium-high heat. Add the sweet potato, onion, paprika, bell pepper, and salt, and cook for about 10 minutes, stirring frequently, or until the potatoes start to soften. 2. Add the kale and garlic, stirring to combine, and cook until the kale begins to wilt, about 3 minutes. 3. Reduce the heat to low. With a spoon or spatula, create 4 pockets for the eggs in the sweet potato mixture. Crack 1 egg into each pocket. Cover the skillet and cook until the yolk is slightly runny and the egg whites are set, about 5 minutes. 4. Remove from the heat and season with the pepper. Serve as is, or with your favorite salsa, if desired. Store any leftovers in an airtight container in the refrigerator for up to 5 days.

Per Serving: Calories 268; Fat 14.2g; Sodium 280mg; Carbs 26.98g; Fiber 4.5g; Sugar 5.66g; Protein 9.22g

Shakshuka

Prep Time: 5 minutes | Cook Time: 20 minutes | Serves: 4

2 tablespoons extra-virgin olive oil

1 cup chopped shallots

1 cup chopped red bell peppers

1 cup finely diced potato

1 teaspoon garlic powder

1 (14.5-ounce) can diced tomatoes, drained

¼ teaspoon turmeric

¼ teaspoon paprika

¼ teaspoon ground cardamom

4 large eggs

¼ cup chopped fresh cilantro

1. Preheat the oven to 350°F. 2. In an oven-safe sauté pan or skillet over medium-high heat, heat the olive oil and sauté the shallots, stirring occasionally, for approximately 3 minutes, until fragrant. Add the potato, bell peppers, and garlic powder. Cook, uncovered, for 10 minutes, stirring every 2 minutes. 3. Add the tomatoes, paprika, turmeric, and cardamom to the skillet and mix well. Once bubbly, remove from the heat and crack the eggs into the skillet so the yolks are facing up. 4. Put the skillet in the oven and cook for another 5 to 10 minutes, until eggs are cooked to your preference. 5. Garnish with the cilantro and serve.

Per Serving: Calories 194; Fat 11.96g; Sodium 194mg; Carbs 14.04g; Fiber 3.9g; Sugar 4.91g; Protein 8.48g

Homemade Marinara Eggs with Parsley

Prep Time: 5 minutes | Cook Time: 15 minutes | Serves: 6

1 tablespoon extra-virgin olive oil

1 cup chopped onion (about ½ medium onion)

2 garlic cloves, minced (about 1 teaspoon)

2 (14.5-ounce) cans Italian diced tomatoes, undrained, no salt

added

6 large eggs

½ cup chopped fresh flat-leaf (Italian) parsley

1. In a large skillet over medium-high heat, heat the oil. Add the onion and cook for 5 minutes, stirring occasionally. Add the garlic and cook for 1 minute. 2. Pour the tomatoes with their juices over the onion mixture and cook until bubbling, 2 to 3 minutes. While waiting for the tomato mixture to bubble, crack one egg into a small custard cup or a coffee mug. 3. When the tomato mixture bubbles, lower the heat to medium. Then make six indentations in the tomato mixture with a large spoon. Gently pour the first cracked egg into one indentation and repeat, cracking the remaining eggs, one at a time, into the custard cup and pouring one into each indentation. Cover the skillet and cook for 6 to 7 minutes, or until the eggs are done to your liking, 6 minutes for soft-cooked or 7 minutes for harder cooked. 4. When done, top with the parsley and serve.

Per Serving: Calories 116; Fat 7.25g; Sodium 82mg; Carbs 5.88g; Fiber 1.9g; Sugar 3.12g; Protein 7.33g

California Breakfast Egg White Scramble

Prep Time: 20 minutes | Cook Time: 5 minutes | Serves: 4

10 large egg whites

1 tablespoon chopped fresh parsley

1 teaspoon chopped fresh basil

½ teaspoon chopped fresh thyme

Sea salt

Pinch freshly ground black pepper

1 tablespoon olive oil

1 ripe avocado, pitted, peeled, and chopped

1 cup halved cherry tomatoes, at room temperature

1 scallion, both white and green parts, thinly sliced on the bias

2 tablespoons chopped fresh cilantro

1 tablespoon minced jalapeño

1. In a medium bowl, stir together the egg whites, basil, parsley, and thyme and season with the salt and pepper. 2. In a large skillet, heat the olive oil over medium heat. Add the egg mixture into the skillet and swirl the pan lightly. Scramble the eggs until cooked through but still moist, about 5 minutes. 3. Spoon the eggs onto a platter and top with the avocado, tomatoes, cilantro, scallion, and jalapeño. Serve.

Per Serving: Calories 180; Fat 11.35g; Sodium 433mg; Carbs 10.11g; Fiber 5.6g; Sugar 4.44g; Protein 11.4g

Kale Pomegranate Smoothie

Prep Time: 5 minutes | Cook Time: 0 minute | Serves: 2

1 cup pure pomegranate juice (no sugar added)

1 cup frozen berries

1 cup coarsely chopped kale

2 tablespoons chia seeds

3 Medjool dates, pitted and coarsely chopped

Pinch ground cinnamon

1. In a blender, add the pomegranate juice, chia seeds, dates, berries, kale, and cinnamon and pulse until smooth. Pour into the glasses and serve.

Per Serving: Calories 278; Fat 4.96g; Sodium 18mg; Carbs 60.36g; Fiber 13g; Sugar 43.14g; Protein 5.54g

Asparagus and Cherry Tomato Omelets

Prep Time: 10 minutes | Cook Time: 20 minutes | Serves: 4

2 tablespoons olive oil, divided

12 asparagus spears, trimmed and cut into 2-inch pieces

1 cup shredded spinach

1 cup halved cherry tomatoes

1 scallion, both white and green parts, thinly sliced on the bias

8 large eggs

1 teaspoon chopped fresh basil

1 teaspoon chopped fresh parsley

Sea salt

Freshly ground black pepper

1. In a medium skillet, heat 2 teaspoons of olive oil over medium-high heat. 2. Sauté the asparagus, tomatoes, spinach, and scallion until tender, about 5 minutes. Remove from the skillet and set aside. 3. In a medium bowl, beat together the eggs, basil, and parsley. Season lightly with the salt and pepper. 4. Wipe the skillet out and add 2 teaspoons of olive oil. Add half of the egg mixture into the skillet and cook, without stirring, until edges are set. Using a spatula, lift the edges and let the uncooked eggs flow underneath. Repeat this process until the eggs are just cooked through, about 4 minutes. 5. Spoon half of the asparagus mixture on half of the omelet and flip the other side of the omelet over the filling. Transfer the omelet to a plate. 6. Repeat steps 4 and 5 with the remaining egg mixture and asparagus mixture to make another omelet. 7. When done, cut the omelets in half and serve.

Per Serving: Calories 223; Fat 16.44g; Sodium 442mg; Carbs 4.8g; Fiber 1.8g; Sugar 2.38g; Protein 14.28g

Baked Mushroom and Spinach Egg Cups

Prep Time: 5 minutes | Cook Time: 15 minutes | Serves: 6

Olive oil cooking spray

6 large eggs

1 garlic clove, minced

½ teaspoon salt

½ teaspoon black pepper

Pinch red pepper flakes

8 ounces baby bella mushrooms, sliced

1 cup fresh baby spinach

2 scallions, white parts and green parts, diced

1. Preheat the air fryer to 320°F. Lightly coat the inside of six silicone muffin cups or a six-cup muffin tin with the olive oil cooking spray. 2. In a large bowl, beat together the eggs, salt, garlic, pepper, and red pepper flakes for 1 to 2 minutes, or until well combined. 3. Fold in the mushrooms, spinach, and scallions. 4. Divide the mixture equally among the muffin cups. 5. Place the muffin cups into the air fryer and bake for 12 to 15 minutes, or until the eggs are set. 6. When done, remove the muffin cups and allow to cool for 5 minutes before serving.

Per Serving: Calories 85; Fat 4.99g; Sodium 272mg; Carbs 2.53g; Fiber 0.7g; Sugar 1.09g; Protein 7.75g

Sweet Potato Hash with Mushrooms

Prep Time: 15 minutes | Cook Time: 18 minutes | Serves: 6

2 medium sweet potatoes, peeled and cut into 1-inch cubes

½ green bell pepper, diced

½ red onion, diced

4 ounces baby bella mushrooms, diced

2 tablespoons olive oil

1 garlic clove, minced

½ teaspoon salt

½ teaspoon black pepper

½ tablespoon chopped fresh rosemary

1. Preheat the air fryer to 380°F. 2. In a large bowl, toss all ingredients together until the vegetables are well coated and seasonings distributed. 3. Pour the vegetables into the air fryer basket in an even layer and cook for 9 minutes. 4. Toss or flip the vegetables and continue to cook for 9 minutes more. 5. When done, transfer to a serving bowl or individual plates and enjoy.

Per Serving: Calories 89; Fat 4.67g; Sodium 209mg; Carbs 11.1g; Fiber 1.8g; Sugar 3.85g; Protein 1.51g

Egg in a "Pepper Hole" with Avocado Salsa

Prep Time: 15 minutes | Cook Time: 5 minutes | Serves: 4

4 bell peppers, any color

1 tablespoon extra-virgin olive oil

8 large eggs

¾ teaspoon kosher salt, divided

¼ teaspoon freshly ground black pepper, divided

1 avocado, peeled, pitted, and diced

¼ cup red onion, diced

¼ cup fresh basil, chopped

Juice of ½ lime

1. Remove stems and seeds from bell peppers. Cut 2 (2-inch-thick) rings from each pepper. Chop the remaining bell pepper into the small dice and set aside. 2. In a large skillet over medium heat, heat the olive oil. Add 4 bell pepper rings and crack 1 egg in the middle of each ring. Season with ⅛ teaspoon black pepper and ¼ teaspoon salt. Cook until the egg whites are mostly set but the yolks are still runny, 2 to 3 minutes. Gently turn and cook 1 minute more for over easy. Transfer the egg–bell pepper rings to a platter or onto plates and repeat with the remaining 4 bell pepper rings. 3. In a medium bowl, combine the avocado, basil, onion, reserved diced bell pepper, lime juice, the remaining ¼ teaspoon kosher salt, and the remaining ⅛ teaspoon black pepper. Divide among the 4 plates. Serve and enjoy.

Per Serving: Calories 287; Fat 20.65g; Sodium 583mg; Carbs 12.21g; Fiber 5.1g; Sugar 4.91g; Protein 15.32g

Tofu Scramble

Prep Time: 5 minutes | Cook Time: 10 minutes | Serves: 2

1 (14-ounce) block extra-firm tofu, drained

2 teaspoons olive oil

½ onion, chopped

½ red bell pepper, seeded and chopped

1 teaspoon minced garlic

2 tablespoons nutritional yeast

¼ teaspoon ground turmeric (optional)

Freshly ground black pepper

1. Crumble the drained tofu into a small bowl. 2. In a large skillet, heat the oil over medium-high heat and sauté the onion, bell pepper, and garlic for about 3 minutes, until softened. 3. Add the tofu and sauté for about 4 minutes, until heated through. Stir in the nutritional yeast and turmeric (if using) and toss until the tofu is well coated. 4. Season with the pepper and serve.

Per Serving: Calories 241; Fat 16.19g; Sodium 19mg; Carbs 8.64g; Fiber 1.7g; Sugar 2.79g; Protein 20.33g

Fried Eggs with Garlic Swiss Chard and Bell Pepper

Prep Time: 10 minutes | Cook Time: 11-13 minutes | Serves: 4

2 tablespoons extra-virgin olive oil

5 garlic cloves, minced

2 pounds Swiss chard, stemmed, 1 cup stems chopped fine, leaves sliced into ½-inch-wide strips

1 small red bell pepper, stemmed, seeded, and cut into ¼-inch

pieces

Pinch salt

⅛ teaspoon red pepper flakes

4 large eggs

Lemon wedges

1. In a 12-inch nonstick skillet over medium-low heat, heat 1 tablespoon oil and garlic, stirring occasionally, until the garlic is light golden, 3 to 5 minutes. Increase the heat to high, add the chard stems, then the chard leaves, a handful at a time, and cook until wilted, about 2 minutes. Stir in the bell pepper, salt, and pepper flakes and cook, stirring often, until the chard is tender and peppers are softened, about 3 minutes. Transfer to a colander set in bowl and let drain while preparing the eggs; discard the liquid. Wipe the skillet clean with paper towels. 2. Crack 2 eggs into a small bowl. Repeat with the remaining 2 eggs in the second bowl. Heat the remaining 1 tablespoon oil in a now-empty skillet over medium-high heat until shimmering; quickly swirl to coat the skillet. Working quickly, pour one bowl of eggs in one side of skillet and the second bowl of eggs in other side. Cover and cook for 1 minute. 3. Remove the skillet from the heat and let sit, covered, 15 to 45 seconds for runny yolks (white around edge of yolk will be barely opaque), 45 to 60 seconds for soft but set yolks, and about 2 minutes for medium-set yolks. 4. Divide the chard mixture between individual plates and top with the eggs. Serve immediately with the lemon wedges.

Per Serving: Calories 188; Fat 12.07g; Sodium 846mg; Carbs 12.05g; Fiber 4.1g; Sugar 3.8g; Protein 10.83g

Garlicky Brussels Sprout Hash and Eggs

Prep Time: 15 minutes | Cook Time: 15 minutes | Serves: 4

3 teaspoons extra-virgin olive oil, divided

1 pound Brussels sprouts, sliced

2 garlic cloves, thinly sliced

¼ teaspoon salt

Juice of 1 lemon

4 eggs

1. In a large skillet, heat 1½ teaspoons oil over medium heat. Add the Brussels sprouts and toss. Cook, stirring regularly, for 6 to 8 minutes until browned and softened. Add the garlic and continue cooking until fragrant, about 1 minute. Season with the salt and lemon juice. Transfer to a serving dish. 2. In the same pan, heat the remaining 1½ teaspoons oil over medium-high heat. Crack the eggs into the pan and fry for 2 to 4 minutes. Flip and continue to cook to your desired doneness. Serve over the bed of hash.

Per Serving: Calories 146; Fat 7.94g; Sodium 237mg; Carbs 11.79g; Fiber 4.4g; Sugar 2.98g; Protein 9.5g

Turkey Breakfast Sausage Patties

Prep Time: 10 minutes | Cook Time: 10 minutes | Serves: 8

1 pound lean ground turkey

½ teaspoon salt

½ teaspoon dried sage

½ teaspoon dried thyme

½ teaspoon freshly ground black pepper

¼ teaspoon ground fennel seeds

1 teaspoon extra-virgin olive oil

1. In a large mixing bowl, add the ground turkey, sage, thyme, salt, pepper, and fennel. Mix well. 2. Shape the meat mixture into 8 small, round patties. 3. In a skillet over medium-high heat, heat the olive oil. Cook the patties in the skillet for 3 to 4 minutes on each side until browned and cooked through. 4. Serve warm, or store in an airtight container in the refrigerator for up to 3 days or in the freezer for up to 1 month.

Per Serving: Calories 91; Fat 5.31g; Sodium 185mg; Carbs 0.2g; Fiber 0.1g; Sugar 0g; Protein 10.66g

Sweet Potato Hash with Turkey Sausage Patties

Prep Time: 10 minutes | Cook Time: 25 minutes | Serves: 4

1 tablespoon extra-virgin olive oil

2 medium sweet potatoes, cut into ½-inch dice

½ recipe Turkey Breakfast Sausage Patties

1 small onion, chopped

½ red bell pepper, seeded and chopped

2 garlic cloves, minced

Chopped fresh parsley, for garnish

1. In a large skillet, heat the oil over medium-high heat. Add the sweet potatoes and cook, stirring occasionally, for 12 to 15 minutes or until they brown and begin to soften. 2. Add the turkey sausage in bulk, bell pepper, onion, and garlic. Cook for 5 to 6 minutes until the turkey sausage is cooked through and the vegetables soften. 3. Garnish with the parsley and serve warm.

Per Serving: Calories 215; Fat 8.86g; Sodium 193mg; Carbs 21.49g; Fiber 2.9g; Sugar 1.9g; Protein 13.23g

Easy Poached Eggs

Nonstick cooking spray

4 large eggs

1. Lightly spray 4 cups of a 7-count silicone egg bite mold with nonstick cooking spray. Crack each egg into a sprayed cup. 2. Add 1 cup of water into the electric pressure cooker. Place a wire rack into the pot and place the egg bite mold on the rack. 3. Close and lock the lid of the pressure cooker. Set the valve to sealing. 4. Cook on high pressure for 5 minutes. 5. When the cooking is complete, hit Cancel and quick release the pressure. 6. Once the pin drops, unlock and remove the lid. 7. Run a small rubber spatula or spoon around each egg and carefully remove from the mold. The whites should be cooked, but the yolks should be runny.

8. Serve immediately.

Per Serving: Calories 72; Fat 4.81g; Sodium 71mg; Carbs 0.38g; Fiber 0g; Sugar 0.19g; Protein 6.28g

Chapter 2 Vegetarian Mains

Roasted Tempeh and Vegetable Power Bowl

8 ounces tempeh, cut into ½-inch pieces

8 ounces Brussels sprouts, trimmed and halved

1 medium sweet potato, peeled and chopped

½ red onion, sliced

¼ cup tamari

2 tablespoons apple cider vinegar

2 teaspoons paprika

¼ cup extra-virgin olive oil, divided

2 cups finely chopped collard greens, stemmed

1 medium avocado, peeled, pitted, and sliced

1 cup Classic Hummus, or store-bought

1. In a large bowl, mix the tempeh, Brussels sprouts, onion, tamari, vinegar, sweet potato, paprika, and 3 tablespoons of olive oil. Cover and refrigerate for at least 30 minutes. 2. Preheat the oven to 400°F. Line a baking sheet with a silicone baking mat or parchment paper. 3. Remove the tempeh and vegetables from the marinade and spread on the prepared baking sheet. Discard the marinade. Roast for 25 minutes, or until the vegetables are tender. 4. Meanwhile, in a medium skillet over medium heat, sauté the collard greens in the remaining 1 tablespoon olive oil until bright green, about 3 minutes. Divide it between four bowls. When the vegetables and tempeh are done, divide them between the four bowls as well. Top each bowl with a quarter of the avocado slices and ¼ cup hummus. 5. Refrigerate the roasted vegetables and tempeh in an airtight container separate from the rest of the ingredients for up to 5 days.

Per Serving: Calories 696; Fat 42.37g; Sodium 1343mg; Carbs 59.38g; Fiber 19.7g; Sugar 11.33g; Protein 28.81g

Baked Sweet Potato, Chickpea, and Zucchini

1 large sweet potato, peeled and cut into ½-inch pieces

2 (15-ounce) cans chickpeas, drained, rinsed, and patted dry

1 medium zucchini, sliced

1 medium red bell pepper, seeded and sliced

½ yellow onion, sliced

2 garlic cloves, minced

2 tablespoons extra-virgin olive oil

1 teaspoon paprika

1 teaspoon Italian seasoning

½ teaspoon salt

¼ teaspoon freshly ground black pepper

1. Preheat the oven to 425°F. Line a baking sheet with a silicone baking mat or parchment paper. 2. In a large bowl, toss together the sweet potato, zucchini, bell pepper, chickpeas, onion, garlic, paprika, Italian seasoning, salt, olive oil, and pepper. Place the mixture on the prepared baking sheet in a single layer. If needed, use two baking sheets to spread them out evenly. Bake for 25 minutes, stirring halfway through, or until the potatoes are tender and the vegetables have reached your desired level of crispiness. Serve hot. 3. Refrigerate the leftovers in an airtight container for up to 5 days.

Per Serving: Calories 277; Fat 9.79g; Sodium 591mg; Carbs 39.58g; Fiber 9.9g; Sugar 10.38g; Protein 9.66g

Vegetable Kebabs

Prep Time: 15 minutes | Cook Time: 15 minutes | Serves: 4

4 medium red onions, peeled and sliced into 6 wedges

4 medium zucchini, cut into 1-inch-thick slices

4 bell peppers, cut into 2-inch squares

2 yellow bell peppers, cut into 2-inch squares

2 orange bell peppers, cut into 2-inch squares

2 beefsteak tomatoes, cut into quarters

3 tablespoons Herbed Oil

1. Preheat the oven or grill to medium-high or 350°F. 2. Thread 1 piece of red onion, zucchini, different colored bell peppers, and tomatoes onto a skewer. Repeat until the skewer is full of vegetables, up to 2 inches away from the skewer end, and continue until all skewers are complete. 3. Place the skewers on a baking sheet and cook in the oven for 10 minutes or grill for 5 minutes on each side. The vegetables will be done with they reach your desired crunch or softness. 4. Remove the skewers from heat and drizzle with the Herbed Oil.

Per Serving: Calories 341; Fat 28.14g; Sodium 105mg; Carbs 22.12g; Fiber 5g; Sugar 10.37g; Protein 5.42g

Israeli Eggplant with Chickpea and Mint

Prep Time: 5 minutes | Cook Time: 20 minutes | Serves: 6

Nonstick cooking spray

1 medium globe eggplant (about 1 pound), stem removed

1 tablespoon extra-virgin olive oil

2 tablespoons freshly squeezed lemon juice (from about 1 small lemon)

2 tablespoons balsamic vinegar

1 teaspoon ground cumin

¼ teaspoon kosher or sea salt

1 (15-ounce) can chickpeas, drained and rinsed

1 cup sliced sweet onion (about ½ medium Walla Walla or Vidalia onion)

¼ cup loosely packed chopped or torn mint leaves

1 tablespoon sesame seeds, toasted if desired

1 garlic clove, finely minced (about ½ teaspoon)

1. Place an oven rack about 4 inches below the broiler element. Turn the oven broiler to the highest setting to preheat. Spray a large rimmed baking sheet with nonstick cooking spray. 2. On a cutting board, slice the eggplant lengthwise into four slices (each about ½- to ⅝-inch thick). Place the eggplant slices on the prepared baking sheet. Set aside. 3. In a small bowl, whisk together the oil, cumin, lemon juice, vinegar, and salt. Brush or drizzle both sides of the eggplant slices with 2 tablespoons lemon dressing. Reserve the remaining dressing. 4. Broil the eggplant directly under the heating element for 4 minutes, flip, and broil for an additional 4 minutes, until golden brown. 5. While the eggplant is broiling, combine the chickpeas, sesame seeds, onion, mint, and garlic in a serving bowl. Add the reserved dressing and gently mix to incorporate all the ingredients. 6. When the eggplant is done, using tongs, transfer the slices from the baking sheet onto a cooling rack and cool for 3 minutes. Once slightly cooled, arrange the eggplant on a cutting board and cut each piece crosswise into ½-inch strips. 7. Place the eggplant in the serving bowl with the onion mixture. Gently toss everything together and serve warm or at room temperature.

Per Serving: Calories 122; Fat 4.24g; Sodium 193mg; Carbs 18.22g; Fiber 5.5g; Sugar 6.69g; Protein 4.39g

Healthy Cannellini Bean Lettuce Wraps

Prep Time: 10 minutes | Cook Time: 10 minutes | Serves: 4

1 tablespoon extra-virgin olive oil

½ cup diced red onion (about ¼ onion)

¾ cup chopped fresh tomatoes (about 1 medium tomato)

¼ teaspoon freshly ground black pepper

1 (15-ounce) can cannellini or great northern beans, drained

and rinsed

¼ cup finely chopped fresh curly parsley

½ cup Lemony Garlic Hummus or ½ cup prepared hummus

8 romaine lettuce leaves

1. In a large skillet over medium heat, heat the oil. Add the onion and cook for 3 minutes, stirring occasionally. Add the pepper and tomatoes and cook for another 3 minutes, stirring occasionally. Add the beans and cook for another 3 minutes, stirring occasionally. Remove from the heat and mix in the parsley. 2. Spread 1 tablespoon hummus on each lettuce leaf. Evenly spread the warm bean mixture evenly in the center of each lettuce leaf. Fold one side of the lettuce leaf lengthwise over the filling, then fold over the other side to make a wrap, and serve.

Per Serving: Calories 228; Fat 6.71g; Sodium 271mg; Carbs 33.25g; Fiber 8.4g; Sugar 3.7g; Protein 10.58g

Rosated Cauliflower Steaks with Eggplant Relish

Prep Time: 5 minutes | Cook Time: 25 minutes | Serves: 4

2 small heads cauliflower (about 3 pounds)

¼ teaspoon kosher or sea salt

¼ teaspoon smoked paprika

Extra-virgin olive oil, divided

1 recipe Eggplant Relish Spread or 1 container store-bought baba ghanoush

1. Place a large, rimmed baking sheet in the oven. Preheat the oven to 400°F with the pan inside. 2. Stand one head of cauliflower on a cutting board, stem-end down. With a long chef's knife, slice down through the very center of the head, including the stem. Starting at the cut edge, measure about 1 inch and cut one thick slice from each cauliflower half, including as much of the stem as possible, to make two cauliflower "steaks." Reserve the remaining cauliflower for another use. Repeat with the second cauliflower head. 3. Dry each steak well with a clean towel. Sprinkle the salt and smoked paprika evenly over both sides of each cauliflower steak. 4. In a large skillet over medium-high heat, heat 2 tablespoons of oil. When the oil is very hot, add two cauliflower steaks to the pan and cook for about 3 minutes, until golden and crispy. Flip and cook for 2 more minutes. Transfer the steaks to a plate. Use a pair of tongs to hold a paper towel and wipe out the pan to remove most of the hot oil (which will contain a few burnt bits of cauliflower). Repeat the cooking process with the remaining 2 tablespoons of oil and the remaining two steaks. 5. Using oven mitts, carefully remove the baking sheet from the oven and arrange the cauliflower on the baking sheet. Roast in the oven for 12 to 15 minutes, until the cauliflower steaks are just fork tender; they will still be somewhat firm. Serve the steaks with the Eggplant Relish Spread, baba ghanoush, or the homemade ketchup.

Per Serving: Calories 239; Fat 10.04g; Sodium 1524mg; Carbs 34.02g; Fiber 12.9g; Sugar 15.96g; Protein 9.44g

Healthy Greek Roasted Vegetable Bowl

Prep Time: 15 minutes | Cook Time: 40 minutes | Serves: 4

1 butternut squash, peeled, seeded, and cut into 1-inch chunks

1 celery root, peeled and cut into 1-inch chunks

2 carrots, peeled and cut into 1-inch chunks

2 parsnips, peeled and cut into 1-inch chunks

1 tablespoon olive oil

Sea salt

Freshly ground black pepper

1 cup shredded spinach

½ cup chopped marinated artichoke hearts

¼ cup chopped oil-packed sun-dried tomatoes

2 tablespoons pitted, sliced Kalamata olives

Juice of 1 lemon

2 tablespoons chopped fresh basil

1. Preheat the oven to 400°F. Line a baking sheet with parchment paper. 2. In a large bowl, toss together the squash, carrots, parsnips, celery root, and olive oil until coated. Season with the salt and pepper. 3. Lay the vegetables flat on the baking sheet and roast until tender and lightly caramelized, turning once, about 40 minutes. 4. Divide the roasted vegetables between bowls and top with the spinach, sun-dried tomatoes, artichoke hearts, and olives. Drizzle the bowls with the lemon juice, top with the basil, and serve.

Per Serving: Calories 171; Fat 5.42g; Sodium 406mg; Carbs 30.58g; Fiber 9g; Sugar 8.64g; Protein 6.68g

Split Pea and Tomato Tabbouleh

Prep Time: 15 minutes | Cook Time: 45 minutes | Serves: 6

1½ cups split peas

4 cups water

2 large tomatoes, seeded and chopped

1 English cucumber, chopped

1 yellow bell pepper, chopped

1 orange bell pepper, chopped

½ red onion, finely chopped

¼ cup chopped fresh cilantro

Juice of 1 lime

1 teaspoon ground cumin

½ teaspoon ground coriander

Pinch red pepper flakes

Sea salt

Freshly ground black pepper

1. In a large saucepan, combine the split peas and water over medium-high heat and bring to a boil. Reduce the heat to low and simmer, uncovered, until the peas are tender, 40 to 45 minutes. Drain the peas and rinse in the cold water to cool. 2. Transfer the peas to a large bowl and add the tomatoes, bell peppers, onion, cucumber, cilantro, lime juice, coriander, cumin, and red pepper flakes. Toss to mix well. Place the mixture in the refrigerator for at least 1 hour to let the flavors mesh. Season with the pepper and salt and serve.

Per Serving: Calories 92; Fat 0.57g; Sodium 204mg; Carbs 17.96g; Fiber 5.8g; Sugar 4.4g; Protein 5.53g

Oven Roasted Vegetable Mélange

Prep Time: 20 minutes | Cook Time: 25 minutes | Serves: 4

½ cauliflower head, cut into small florets

½ broccoli head, cut into small florets

2 zucchini, cut into ½-inch pieces

2 cups halved mushrooms

2 red, orange, or yellow bell peppers, cut into 1-inch pieces

1 sweet potato, cut into 1-inch pieces

1 red onion, cut into wedges

3 tablespoons olive oil

2 teaspoons minced garlic

1 teaspoon chopped fresh thyme

Sea salt

Freshly ground black pepper

1. Preheat the oven to 400°F. Line a baking sheet with parchment paper and set aside. 2. In a large bowl, toss the cauliflower, mushrooms, broccoli, bell peppers, zucchini, sweet potato, onion, garlic, olive oil, and thyme until well mixed. Lay the vegetables flat on the baking sheet and season lightly with the salt and pepper. 3. Roast until the vegetables are tender and lightly caramelized, stirring occasionally, 20 to 25 minutes. Serve and enjoy.

Per Serving: Calories 181; Fat 10.84g; Sodium 339mg; Carbs 19.29g; Fiber 4.5g; Sugar 7.85g; Protein 4.94g

Perfect Patatas Bravas

Prep Time: 10 minutes | Cook Time: 55 minutes | Serves: 4-6

5 medium russet potatoes

⅓ cup extra-virgin olive oil

2 teaspoons salt

1 teaspoon paprika

¼ teaspoon freshly ground black pepper

1 recipe Aioli

1. Preheat the oven to 375°F. 2. Wash the potatoes, place them on a baking sheet, and bake until tender, about 35 to 45 minutes. 3. Allow to cool for several minutes until you can handle them, and cut them into 8 wedges. Place the wedges in a bowl. 4. Increase the heat to 400°F. 5. Add the olive oil, paprika, salt, and pepper, and mix gently to coat the wedges with the spice mix without mashing the potatoes. 6. Arrange the potatoes in a single layer on a baking sheet. 7. Return the baking sheet with potatoes to the oven and roast for 10 to 15 minutes, or until the potatoes are golden brown and crispy. 8. Serve warm with Aioli.

Per Serving: Calories 577; Fat 48.86g; Sodium 1179mg; Carbs 33.06g; Fiber 2.5g; Sugar 1.24g; Protein 4.41g

Hearty Ratatouille

2 Japanese eggplants, cut into ½-inch-thick slices

1 teaspoon salt

¼ cup extra-virgin olive oil

2 garlic cloves, sliced

1 onion, sliced

1 red bell pepper, cored, seeded, and cut into ½-inch pieces

4 medium tomatoes, cored and cut into ½-inch pieces

2 large zucchini, cut into ½-inch slices

¼ cup chopped fresh flatleaf parsley

1 tablespoon capers

1 teaspoon herbes de Provence or rosemary

1 teaspoon salt

¼ teaspoon freshly ground black pepper

1. Sprinkle the Japanese eggplant with the salt and set aside in a colander in the sink while you prepare the rest of the vegetables. This draws the excess water from the eggplant. 2. In a large Dutch oven or a heavy pot with a lid, heat the olive oil over high heat. 3. Add the garlic, onion, and bell pepper and sauté for about 8 minutes or until the vegetables are wilted. 4. Dry the eggplant with a paper towel and add the eggplant, tomatoes, and zucchini to the pot. 5. Bring to a simmer and cook, stirring the vegetables for about 5 minutes. Cover the pot, reduce the heat to medium, and continue to cook on a low simmer for about 30 minutes or until the vegetables are very soft and tender. 6. Remove the pot from the heat and add the parsley, herbes de Provence, salt, capers, and pepper. 7. Spoon into a serving dish and serve. 8. Store in an airtight container in the refrigerator for about 1 week or in the freezer for several months.

Per Serving: Calories 148; Fat 9.6g; Sodium 819mg; Carbs 15.56g; Fiber 6.9g; Sugar 9.1g; Protein 3g

Sautéed Greens

2 tablespoons olive oil

8 cups stemmed and coarsely chopped spinach, kale, collard greens, or Swiss chard

Juice of ½ lemon

Sea salt

Freshly ground black pepper

1. In a large skillet, heat the olive oil over medium-high heat. Add greens and cook, stirring with tongs, until wilted and tender, 8 to 10 minutes. 2. Remove the skillet from the heat and squeeze in the lemon juice, tossing to coat evenly. Season with the pepper and salt and serve.

Per Serving: Calories 76; Fat 7.01g; Sodium 338mg; Carbs 2.78g; Fiber 1.4g; Sugar 0.41g; Protein 1.77g

Tunisian Eggs with Tomatoes and Peppers

Prep Time: 10 minutes | Cook Time: 15 minutes | Serves: 4

2 tablespoons extra-virgin olive oil

1 onion, thinly sliced

1 tablespoon paprika

1 teaspoon whole cumin seeds

1 garlic clove, minced

3 large tomatoes, cored and diced

1 large red bell pepper, seeded and chopped

1 large green bell pepper, seeded and chopped

1 tablespoon harissa

½ cup water or vegetable broth

1 teaspoon salt

4 eggs

2 tablespoons fresh flatleaf parsley, chopped

1. Heat the olive oil in a large skillet over high heat. 2. Add the onion, paprika, and cumin seeds and sauté 5 minutes to toast the spices. 3. Add the garlic, bell peppers, harissa, tomatoes, water or broth, and salt. Bring to a simmer and cook 5 to 7 minutes to thicken the sauce. 4. Using the back of a spoon, make 4 indentations in the sauce and carefully crack one egg into each indentation. 5. Cover the pan and cook 2 to 3 minutes to set the eggs. 6. Sprinkle the parsley over the cooked eggs and serve. 7. The sauce for this dish can be made ahead and stored in the fridge for 1 week or the freezer for several months.

Per Serving: Calories 166; Fat 11.61g; Sodium 986mg; Carbs 9.73g; Fiber 2.8g; Sugar 5.49g; Protein 7.58g

Rosemary Roasted Red Potatoes

Prep Time: 5 minutes | Cook Time: 20 minutes | Serves: 6

1 pound red potatoes, quartered

¼ cup olive oil

½ teaspoon kosher salt

¼ teaspoon black pepper

1 garlic clove, minced

4 rosemary sprigs

1. Preheat the air fryer to 360°F. 2. In a large bowl, toss the potatoes with the olive oil, pepper, salt, and garlic until well coated. 3. Pour the potatoes into the air fryer basket, top with the rosemary sprigs, and roast for 10 minutes. 4. Toss the potatoes and roast for 10 minutes more. 5. Remove the rosemary sprigs and serve. Season with the additional salt and pepper, if needed.

Per Serving: Calories 134; Fat 9.14g; Sodium 208mg; Carbs 12.36g; Fiber 1.4g; Sugar 0.98g; Protein 1.49g

Simple Roasted Radishes

Prep Time: 5 minutes | Cook Time: 18 minutes | Serves: 4

1 pound radishes, ends trimmed if needed

2 tablespoons olive oil

½ teaspoon sea salt

1. Preheat the air fryer to 360°F. 2. In a large bowl, toss the radishes with the olive oil and sea salt. 3. Pour the radishes into the air fryer and cook for 10 minutes. Turn the radishes over and cook for 8 minutes more. 3. Serve and enjoy.

Per Serving: Calories 80; Fat 6.86g; Sodium 315mg; Carbs 4.65g; Fiber 1.8g; Sugar 2.84g; Protein 0.68g

Garlic Zucchini with Red Pepper

Prep Time: 5 minutes | Cook Time: 15 minutes | Serves: 6

2 medium zucchini, cubed

1 red bell pepper, diced

2 garlic cloves, sliced

2 tablespoons olive oil

½ teaspoon salt

1. Preheat the air fryer to 380°F. 2. In a large bowl, mix together the zucchini, bell pepper, garlic, olive oil and salt. 3. Pour the mixture into the air fryer basket and roast for 7 minutes. 4. Shake and roast for 7 to 8 minutes more. 5. Serve and enjoy.

Per Serving: Calories 55; Fat 4.75g; Sodium 200mg; Carbs 3.02g; Fiber 0.8g; Sugar 2.04g; Protein 0.99g

Spiralized Summer Squash

Prep Time: 10 minutes | Cook Time: 20 minutes | Serves: 4

1 (6-inch-long) zucchini

1 (6-inch-long) yellow summer squash

2 teaspoons olive oil

¼ teaspoon salt

Pepper, if desired

1. Heat the oven to 400°F. Line 15×10×1-inch pan with foil. 2. Cut off ends of both squash. Cut the squash with a spiralizer according to manufacturer's directions. Place the squash in the pan, drizzle with the oil, and sprinkle with the salt. Toss to coat and spread squash in single layer. 3. Bake the squash for 8 to 10 minutes or just until tender. Sprinkle with the pepper and serve.

Per Serving: Calories 37; Fat 2.5g; Sodium 150mg; Carbs 3.36g; Fiber 1.1g; Sugar 2.3g; Protein 1.22g

Mexican Cauliflower Rice

Prep Time: 5 minutes | Cook Time: 5 minutes | Serves: 4

3 cups cauliflower florets

1 tablespoon extra-virgin olive oil

½ cup diced onions

⅔ cup sliced tomatoes

1 teaspoon garlic powder

Pinch cayenne pepper

¼ cup chopped fresh cilantro

Juice of ½ lime

⅛ teaspoon salt

⅛ teaspoon freshly ground black pepper

1. In a food processor, pulse the cauliflower a few times until it is in small, rice-like pieces. 2. In a large skillet, heat the olive oil over medium-high heat. Add the cauliflower and onions and sauté until the onions are translucent, 3 to 4 minutes. 3. Add the tomatoes and cook until the tomatoes are broken down, 1 to 2 minutes. Stir in the cayenne pepper and garlic powder and remove from the heat. 4. Stir in the cilantro, lime juice, salt, and pepper. Serve warm.

Per Serving: Calories 66; Fat 3.71g; Sodium 105mg; Carbs 7.7g; Fiber 2.4g; Sugar 3.07g; Protein 2.16g

Braised Turnips in a Creamy Coconut Sauce

Prep Time: 10 minutes | Cook Time: 12 minutes | Serves: 4

1 bunch turnips, with greens

1 tablespoon organic canola oil

½ teaspoon mustard seeds

½ onion, finely chopped

2 tablespoons water

1 teaspoon ground turmeric

½ teaspoon salt

¼ cup coconut milk

1. Remove the leaves from the radishes and cut the turnips into 1-inch chunks. Cut the leaves in half lengthwise, stack them in a pile, and then cut them cross-wise into thin strips. 2. In a large skillet over medium-high heat, heat the oil. Add the mustard seeds and cook until they stop popping. Add the onion and sauté until it starts to soften, 2 to 3 minutes. 3. Add the turnips, water, turmeric, greens, and salt. Cover and reduce the heat to medium. Cook until the turnips are tender, 5 to 7 minutes. 4. Remove the lid and return the heat to medium-high. Cook off any excess liquid that remains in the pan. Add the coconut milk and stir until heated through. Serve.

Per Serving: Calories 109; Fat 7.33g; Sodium 376mg; Carbs 10.53g; Fiber 3g; Sugar 5.76g; Protein 1.73g

Sautéed Green Beans with Garlic and Ginger

Prep Time: 10 minutes | Cook Time: 10 minutes | Serves: 4

1 pound green beans, trimmed

1 tablespoon extra-virgin olive oil

1 shallot, minced

2 garlic cloves, minced

2-inch knob ginger, minced

¼ teaspoon salt

1. Fill a large bowl with ice water and set aside. 2. Bring a large pot of salted water to a boil over high heat. Add the beans and return the water to a boil. Cook until just tender but still bright green, about 3 minutes. Transfer the beans to the ice bath with a slotted spoon. Allow the beans to cool for 3 minutes and transfer them to a colander to drain. Pat the beans dry with paper towels or a clean kitchen towel. 3. In a large skillet, heat the oil over medium heat. Add the garlic, shallot, and ginger and sauté until the garlic turns a light golden brown and the shallot becomes tender. 4. Add the green beans to the skillet and toss until heated through, 2 to 3 minutes. Season with the salt and serve.

Per Serving: Calories 70; Fat 3.64g; Sodium 153mg; Carbs 9.02g; Fiber 3.2g; Sugar 3.93g; Protein 2.25g

Old-Fashioned Sweet Potato Bake with Pecans

Prep Time: 10 minutes | Cook Time: 1 hour 15 minutes | Serves: 8

Nonstick cooking spray

2 pounds sweet potatoes (about 4 medium potatoes)

½ teaspoon ground cinnamon

2 tablespoons freshly squeezed orange juice

2 large eggs

¼ cup chopped pecans

1. Preheat the oven to 350°F. Lightly coat an 8-inch square baking dish with nonstick cooking spray. 2. Fill a large pot with water and bring to a boil over high heat. Add the sweet potatoes, reduce the heat, and slow-boil the potatoes until a fork can be inserted in each potato easily, about 30 minutes. Drain the potatoes and cool. Peel the potatoes. 3. Transfer the potatoes to the bowl of an electric mixer and lightly beat them. Add the cinnamon, orange juice, and eggs. Whip on high until all the ingredients are incorporated and the mixture is slightly fluffy, about 45 seconds. 4. Add the mixture into the prepared baking dish. Bake for 40 minutes. Sprinkle the pecans evenly across the top and bake for another 5 minutes. 5. Serve and enjoy.

Per Serving: Calories 129; Fat 3.56g; Sodium 25mg; Carbs 20.92g; Fiber 2.9g; Sugar 1.38g; Protein 4.18g

Chapter 3 Snacks and Sides

No-Bake Nutty Date Bars

Prep Time: 10 minutes | Cook Time: 0 minute | Serves: 6

1½ cups pitted Medjool dates

1 cup walnuts

½ cup almonds

¼ cup chia seeds

2 tablespoons unsweetened cocoa powder

1 teaspoon vanilla extract

⅛ teaspoon salt

1. Line an 8-inch square baking pan with parchment paper and set it aside. 2. In a food processor or high-powered blender, combine the dates, walnuts, and almonds. Pulse and process until the dates and nuts break down and start to form a ball. Add the chia seeds, vanilla, cocoa powder, and salt. Process until well combined. 3. Transfer the mixture to the prepared baking pan, pressing it evenly into the bottom. Refrigerate for about 2 hours, or until firm. Cut into 12 bars and serve. Store, covered, in the refrigerator for up to 1 week.

Per Serving: Calories 320; Fat 20.75g; Sodium 54mg; Carbs 32.82g; Fiber 7.6g; Sugar 22.42g; Protein 7.39g

Roasted Broccoli and Cauliflower with Turkey Bacon

Prep Time: 15 minutes | Cook Time: 25 minutes | Serves: 4

2 cups chopped broccoli florets

2 cups chopped cauliflower florets

2 tablespoons extra-virgin olive oil

⅛ teaspoon salt

⅛ teaspoon freshly ground black pepper

6 lean turkey bacon slices

2 scallions, green and white parts, sliced

1. Preheat the oven to 400°F. Line a baking sheet with a silicone baking mat or parchment paper and set aside. 2. In a large bowl, combine the broccoli, cauliflower, salt, olive oil, and pepper. Spread the vegetable mixture across the prepared baking sheet and bake in the oven for 10 minutes. 3. Remove the vegetables from the oven and stir. Place the turkey bacon slices on top of the vegetables, return to the oven, and continue to bake for an additional 15 minutes, or until the vegetables and bacon reach your desired level of crispiness. 4. Let the mixture cool slightly and then transfer the broccoli and cauliflower to a serving bowl. Chop the bacon and stir into the vegetables. Garnish with the chopped scallions and serve warm. 5. Refrigerate any leftovers in an airtight container for up to 7 days.

Per Serving: Calories 250; Fat 22.4g; Sodium 293mg; Carbs 6.62g; Fiber 2.5g; Sugar 2.29g; Protein 7.34g

Lemon Roasted Asparagus

1 pound asparagus, ends trimmed

2 tablespoons extra-virgin olive oil

Juice and grated zest of ½ lemon

¼ teaspoon salt

¼ teaspoon freshly ground black pepper

1. Preheat the oven to 400°F. Line a baking sheet with a silicone baking mat or aluminum foil. 2. Place the asparagus on the prepared baking sheet and drizzle with the olive oil, rubbing to fully coat all the spears. 3. Sprinkle with the lemon juice, salt, lemon zest, and pepper. Lightly toss the asparagus to distribute the toppings and then evenly space the spears across the baking sheet. 4. Bake the asparagus in the oven for 12 to 15 minutes, or until tender-crisp. Serve immediately. Store any leftovers in an airtight container in the refrigerator for up to 4 days.

Per Serving: Calories 84; Fat 6.91g; Sodium 148mg; Carbs 4.91g; Fiber 2.4g; Sugar 2.28g; Protein 2.53g

Sautéed Zucchini with Cherry Tomatoes

1 medium zucchini

1 tablespoon extra-virgin olive oil

½ medium yellow onion, diced

1 cup halved cherry tomatoes

2 garlic cloves, minced

¼ teaspoon salt

⅛ teaspoon freshly ground black pepper

1 tablespoon freshly squeezed lemon juice

1 teaspoon grated lemon zest

1. Using a vegetable peeler or mandoline, peel the zucchini lengthwise to form thin ribbons. 2. In a large skillet, heat the olive oil over medium heat. Add the zucchini and onion and cook until they begin to soften, 3 to 5 minutes. Add the garlic, tomatoes, salt, and pepper and cook until the zucchini is tender-crisp and the tomatoes have started to collapse, about 5 minutes. 3. Stir in the lemon juice and cook for 1 more minute. 4. Transfer to a serving dish, garnish with the lemon zest, and serve hot. 5. Refrigerate any leftovers in an airtight container for up to 5 days.

Per Serving: Calories 54; Fat 3.64g; Sodium 152mg; Carbs 5.15g; Fiber 1.2g; Sugar 2.93g; Protein 1.19g

Italian Roasted Vegetables

Prep Time: 15 minutes | Cook Time: 45 minutes | Serves: 6

Nonstick cooking spray

2 eggplants, peeled and sliced ⅛ inch thick

1 zucchini, sliced ¼ inch thick

1 yellow summer squash, sliced ¼ inch thick

2 Roma tomatoes, sliced ⅛ inch thick

¼ cup, plus 2 tablespoons extra-virgin olive oil, divided

1 tablespoon garlic powder

¼ teaspoon dried oregano

¼ teaspoon dried basil

¼ teaspoon salt

Freshly ground black pepper

1. Preheat the oven to 400°F. 2. Spray a 9-by-13-inch baking dish with cooking spray. In the dish, toss the eggplant, squash, zucchini, and tomatoes with 2 tablespoons oil, garlic powder, basil, salt, oregano, and pepper. 3. Standing the vegetables up (like little soldiers), alternate layers of eggplant, zucchini, squash, and Roma tomato. 4. Drizzle the top with the remaining ¼ cup of olive oil. 5. Bake, uncovered, for 40 to 45 minutes, or until vegetables are golden brown.

Per Serving: Calories 62; Fat 1.08g; Sodium 105mg; Carbs 12.76g; Fiber 5.6g; Sugar 7.1g; Protein 2.65g

Garlic-Lemon Hummus

Prep Time: 15 minutes | Cook Time: 0 minute | Serves: 6

1 (15-ounce) can chickpeas, drained and rinsed

4 to 5 tablespoons tahini (sesame seed paste)

4 tablespoons extra-virgin olive oil, divided

2 lemons, juice

1 lemon, zested, divided

1 tablespoon minced garlic

Pinch salt

1. In a food processor, combine the chickpeas, tahini, lemon juice, half of the lemon zest, 2 tablespoons of olive oil, and garlic and blend for up to 1 minute. After 30 seconds of blending, stop and scrape the sides down with a spatula, before blending for another 30 seconds. At this point, you've made hummus! Taste and add salt as desired. Feel free to add 1 teaspoon of water at a time to help thin the hummus to a better consistency. 2. Scoop the hummus into a bowl, drizzle with the remaining 2 tablespoons of olive oil, and remaining lemon zest. 3. Serve and enjoy.

Per Serving: Calories 237; Fat 4.85g; Sodium 296mg; Carbs 13.92g; Fiber 3.7g; Sugar 2.36g; Protein 4.85g

Trail Mix

Prep Time: 5 minutes | Cook Time: 0 minute | Serves: 6

1 cup roughly chopped unsalted walnuts

½ cup roughly chopped salted almonds

½ cup shelled salted pistachios

½ cup roughly chopped apricots

½ cup roughly chopped dates

⅓ cup dried figs, sliced in half

1. In a large zip-top bag, combine the walnuts, pistachios, almonds, apricots, dates, and figs and mix well.

Per Serving: Calories 316; Fat 23.53g; Sodium 103mg; Carbs 23.98g; Fiber 5.6g; Sugar 14.82g; Protein 8.29g

Crunchy Turmeric-Spiced Chickpeas

Prep Time: 15 minutes | Cook Time: 30 minutes | Serves: 4

2 (15-ounce) cans organic chickpeas, drained and rinsed

3 tablespoons extra-virgin olive oil

2 teaspoons Turkish or smoked paprika

2 teaspoons turmeric

½ teaspoon dried oregano

½ teaspoon salt

¼ teaspoon ground ginger

⅛ teaspoon ground white pepper (optional)

1. Preheat the oven to 400°F. Line a baking sheet with parchment paper and set aside. 2. Completely dry the chickpeas. Lay the chickpeas out on a baking sheet, roll them around with paper towels, and allow them to air-dry. I usually let them dry for at least 2½ hours, but can also be left to dry overnight. 3. In a medium bowl, combine the olive oil, turmeric, oregano, paprika, salt, ginger, and white pepper (if using). 4. Add the dry chickpeas to the bowl and toss to combine. 5. Arrange the chickpeas on the prepared baking sheet and cook in the oven for 30 minutes, or until the chickpeas turn golden brown. 5. At 15 minutes, move the chickpeas around on the baking sheet to avoid burning. Check every 10 minutes in case the chickpeas begin to crisp up before the full cooking time has elapsed. 6. Remove from the oven and set them aside to cool.

Per Serving: Calories 274; Fat 13.47g; Sodium 561mg; Carbs 30.9g; Fiber 8.8g; Sugar 5.26g; Protein 9.28g

Crispy Garlic Oven Baked Potatoes

Prep Time: 30 minutes | Cook Time: 30 minutes | Serves: 2

10 ounces golden mini potatoes, halved

4 tablespoons extra-virgin olive oil

2 teaspoons dried, minced garlic

1 teaspoon onion salt

½ teaspoon paprika

¼ teaspoon freshly ground black pepper

¼ teaspoon red pepper flakes

¼ teaspoon dried dill

1. Preheat the oven to 400°F. 2. Soak the potatoes and put in a bowl of ice water for 30 minutes. Change the water if you return and the water is milky. 3. Rinse and dry the potatoes, and put them on a baking sheet. 4. Drizzle the potatoes with the oil and sprinkle with the garlic, onion salt, paprika, red pepper flakes, pepper, and dill. Using tongs or your hands, toss well to coat. 5. Lower the heat to 375°F, add potatoes to the oven, and bake for 20 minutes. 6. At 20 minutes, check and flip the potatoes. Bake for another 10 minutes, or until the potatoes are fork-tender. 7. Serve and enjoy.

Per Serving: Calories 357; Fat 27.31g; Sodium 10mg; Carbs 26.71g; Fiber 3.6g; Sugar 1.33g; Protein 3.26g

Turkish-Spiced Nuts

Prep Time: 10 minutes | Cook Time: 5 minutes | Serves: 4-6

1 tablespoon extra-virgin olive oil

1 cup mixed nuts (walnuts, almonds, cashews, peanuts)

2 tablespoons paprika

1 tablespoon dried mint

½ tablespoon ground cinnamon

½ tablespoon kosher salt

¼ tablespoon garlic powder

¼ teaspoon freshly ground black pepper

⅛ tablespoon ground cumin

1. In a small to medium saucepan, heat the oil on low heat. 2. Once the oil is warm, add the nuts, paprika, salt, mint, cinnamon, garlic powder, pepper, and cumin and stir continually until the spices are well incorporated with the nuts.

Per Serving: Calories 158; Fat 15.32g; Sodium 585mg; Carbs 4.97g; Fiber 2.6g; Sugar 0.77g; Protein 3.47g

Pickled Turnips

Prep Time: 5 minutes | Cook Time: 0 minute | Serves: 4

1 pound turnips, washed well, peeled, and cut into 1-inch batons

1 small beet, roasted, peeled, and cut into 1-inch batons

2 garlic cloves, smashed

1 teaspoon dried Turkish oregano

3 cups warm water

½ cup red wine vinegar

½ cup white vinegar

1. In a jar, combine the turnips, beet, garlic, and oregano. Pour the water and vinegars over the vegetables. Cover, shake well, and put it in the refrigerator. The turnips will be pickled after 1 hour.

Per Serving: Calories 74; Fat 0.15g; Sodium 125mg; Carbs 14.71g; Fiber 2.4g; Sugar 10.09g; Protein 1.52g

Crunchy Orange Chickpeas

Prep Time: 5 minutes | Cook Time: 20 minutes | Serves: 4

1 (15-ounce) can chickpeas, drained and rinsed

2 teaspoons extra-virgin olive oil

¼ teaspoon dried thyme or ½ teaspoon chopped fresh thyme

leaves

⅛ teaspoon kosher or sea salt

Zest of ½ orange (about ½ teaspoon)

1. Preheat the oven to 450°F. 2. Spread the chickpeas on a clean kitchen towel and rub gently until dry. 3. Spread the chickpeas on a large, rimmed baking sheet. Drizzle with the oil and sprinkle with the thyme and salt. Using a Microplane or citrus zester, zest about half of the orange over the chickpeas. Mix well using your hands. 4. Bake for 10 minutes, then open the oven door and, using an oven mitt, give the baking sheet a quick shake, do not removing the sheet from the oven. Bake for 10 minutes more. Taste the chickpeas (carefully!). If they are golden but you think they could be a bit crunchier, bake for 3 minutes more before serving.

Per Serving: Calories 108; Fat 3.83g; Sodium 212mg; Carbs 14.65g; Fiber 4.1g; Sugar 2.54g; Protein 4.48g

Boiled Artichokes with Aioli

Prep Time: 15 minutes | Cook Time: 20 minutes | Serves: 4

2 large artichokes

1 garlic clove, smashed

2 teaspoons salt

½ cup Aioli

1. Using a sharp chef's knife or serrated knife, cut the artichokes in half lengthwise from the stem end through the top. 2. Using a sharp knife, cut the choke out of the artichokes. 3. Place the garlic clove and salt in a large pot and cover with enough water to cover the artichokes by 1 inch. 4. Cover the pot and bring to a boil. Boil for 20 to 30 minutes, or until the artichokes are tender at the stem end. 5. Remove the artichokes to a serving platter and allow to cool. Drain. 6. Serve the artichokes warm or cold. 7. Serve the artichokes with aioli for dipping the leaves, but be sure and eat the stem, too—that's where most the nutrition is. 8. Cooked artichokes will last 1 week, covered, in the refrigerator.

Per Serving: Calories 534; Fat 55.3g; Sodium 1831mg; Carbs 9.81g; Fiber 4.5g; Sugar 0.95g; Protein 3.52g

Sautéed Olives with Garlic

Prep Time: 10 minutes | Cook Time: 5 minutes | Serves: 6-8

2 tablespoons extra-virgin olive oil

2 cups pitted olives (Kalamata and Sicilian or a pitted Greek blend)

⅛ teaspoon red pepper flakes (optional)

1 garlic clove, minced

1 scallion, thinly sliced

½ teaspoon dried rosemary

1 tablespoon slivered Preserved Lemons (optional)

1. Place a medium frying pan over high heat. 2. Add the olive oil, olives, red pepper flakes (if using), and garlic. Sauté for 5 minutes or until the olives start to wilt. 3. Add the scallions, rosemary, and Preserved Lemon (if using). Serve warm. 4. Store any leftovers in the refrigerator for up to 10 days.

Per Serving: Calories 67; Fat 6.61g; Sodium 249mg; Carbs 2.52g; Fiber 1.1g; Sugar 0.13g; Protein 0.38g

Moroccan Zucchini Spread

Prep Time: 10 minutes | Cook Time: 20 minutes | Serves: 4

¼ cup plus 1 tablespoon extra-virgin olive oil, divided, plus more for drizzling

4 large zucchini, cut in half lengthwise

2 teaspoons salt, divided

¼ cup tahini

1 garlic clove, minced

¼ cup lemon juice

½ teaspoon dried oregano

¼ teaspoon cayenne pepper

2 scallions, thinly sliced

1 tablespoon chopped fresh mint

1. Preheat the oven to 375°F. 2. Brush a baking sheet with the olive oil. 3. Brush the zucchini with ¼ cup olive oil and sprinkle with 1 teaspoon salt. Place the zucchini skin side down on the oiled baking sheet. 4. Roast for 15 to 20 minutes or until the zucchini is so soft it can be mashed with a fork. 5. Place the zucchini in a medium bowl and mash with a fork or potato masher. 6. Mix in the tahini, garlic, 1 tablespoon olive oil, 1 teaspoon salt, the lemon juice, oregano, and cayenne. 7. Add the scallions and mint and mix well. 8. Spoon the mixture into a serving bowl, drizzle with the olive oil, and serve warm or at room temperature. 9. The spread will keep 5 days in the refrigerator or in the freezer for several months.

Per Serving: Calories 296; Fat 25.39g; Sodium 1208mg; Carbs 15.35g; Fiber 5.1g; Sugar 8.73g; Protein 6.77g

Sautéed Almonds with Apricots

Prep Time: 10 minutes | Cook Time: 5 minutes | Serves: 4

2 tablespoons extra-virgin olive oil

1 cup blanched (skinless) unsalted almonds

½ teaspoon sea salt

⅛ teaspoon red pepper flakes (optional)

⅛ teaspoon ground cinnamon

½ cup dried apricots, chopped

1. Place a medium frying pan over the high heat. Add the olive oil, almonds, and sea salt and sauté until the almonds are a light golden brown, 5 to 10 minutes. It's important to stir constantly while cooking them since they burn easily. 2. Spoon the hot almonds into a serving dish and add the red pepper flakes (if using), cinnamon, and apricot pieces. 3. Let cool and serve. 4. These nuts can be stored in an airtight container at room temperature 4 or 5 days.

Per Serving: Calories 337; Fat 28.5g; Sodium 293mg; Carbs 17.21g; Fiber 5.4g; Sugar 10.48g; Protein 8.89g

Lemon Shrimp with Garlic Olive Oil Dipping

Prep Time: 5 minutes | Cook Time: 6 minutes | Serves: 4

1 pound medium shrimp, cleaned and deveined

¼ cup plus 2 tablespoons olive oil, divided

Juice of ½ lemon

3 garlic cloves, minced and divided

½ teaspoon salt

¼ teaspoon red pepper flakes

Lemon wedges, for serving (optional)

Marinara sauce, for dipping (optional)

1. Preheat the air fryer to 380°F. 2. In a large bowl, combine the shrimp with 2 tablespoons of the olive oil, as well as the lemon juice, ⅓ minced garlic, salt, and red pepper flakes. Toss to coat the shrimp well. 3. In a small ramekin, combine the remaining ¼ cup of olive oil and the remaining minced garlic. 4. Tear off a 12-by-12-inch sheet of aluminum foil. Pour the shrimp into the center of the foil, then fold the sides up and crimp the edges so that it forms an aluminum foil bowl that is open on top. Place the packet into the air fryer basket. 5. Roast the shrimp for 4 minutes, then open the air fryer, and place the ramekin with oil and garlic in the basket beside the shrimp packet. Cook for 2 more minutes. 6. Transfer the shrimp on a serving plate or platter with the ramekin of garlic olive oil on the side for dipping. You may also serve with the lemon wedges and marinara sauce, if desired.

Per Serving: Calories 223; Fat 14.15g; Sodium 427mg; Carbs 2.06g; Fiber 0.1g; Sugar 0.49g; Protein 23.01g

Red Pepper Tapenade

Prep Time: 5 minutes | Cook Time: 5 minutes | Serves: 4

1 large red bell pepper

2 tablespoons plus 1 teaspoon olive oil, divided

½ cup Kalamata olives, pitted and roughly chopped

1 garlic clove, minced

½ teaspoon dried oregano

1 tablespoon lemon juice

1. Preheat the air fryer to 380°F. 2. Brush the outside of a whole red pepper with 1 teaspoon olive oil and place it inside the air fryer basket. Roast for 5 minutes. 3. Meanwhile, in a medium bowl, combine the remaining 2 tablespoons of olive oil with the olives, oregano, garlic, and lemon juice. 4. Remove the red pepper from the air fryer, then gently slice off the stem and remove the seeds. Roughly chop the roasted pepper into small pieces. 5. Add the red pepper to the olive mixture and stir all together until combined. 6. Serve and enjoy.

Per Serving: Calories 84; Fat 8.4g; Sodium 125mg; Carbs 2.68g; Fiber 0.8g; Sugar 0.68g; Protein 0.45g

Garlic Roasted Tomatoes and Olives

Prep Time: 5 minutes | Cook Time: 20 minutes | Serves: 6

2 cups cherry tomatoes

4 garlic cloves, roughly chopped

½ red onion, roughly chopped

1 cup black olives

1 cup green olives

1 tablespoon fresh basil, minced

1 tablespoon fresh oregano, minced

2 tablespoons olive oil

¼ to ½ teaspoon salt

1. Preheat the air fryer to 380°F. 2. In a large bowl, combine all ingredients and toss together so that the tomatoes and olives are coated well with the olive oil and herbs. 3. Pour the mixture into the air fryer basket and roast for 10 minutes. Stir the mixture well and continue roasting for an additional 10 minutes. 4. Remove from the air fryer, transfer to a serving bowl, and enjoy.

Per Serving: Calories 114; Fat 10.22g; Sodium 609mg; Carbs 6.34g; Fiber 2.6g; Sugar 1.95g; Protein 1.2g

Taco Fries

Prep Time: 10 minutes | Cook Time: 20-25 minutes | Serves: 6

1¼ lb russet or sweet potatoes (2 or 3 potatoes), peeled

2 tablespoons plus 1 teaspoon Salt-Free Taco Seasoning Mix

¼ teaspoon salt

1. Heat the oven to 450°F. Spray 15×10×1-inch pan with cooking spray. 2. Cut the potatoes in half lengthwise. Cut each half lengthwise into 4 wedges (about 1½ inches on the wide side) and place the potatoes cut side down in the pan. Spray the potatoes with cooking spray, turn the potatoes, and spray other side. Sprinkle with the taco seasoning mix and toss until potatoes are evenly coated. Arrange the potatoes in single layer in pan. 3. Bake uncovered for 20 to 25 minutes or until bottoms are crispy. Turn the potatoes. Bake for about 5 minutes longer or until bottoms are crispy. 4. Serve and enjoy.

Per Serving: Calories 97; Fat 0.52g; Sodium 380mg; Carbs 22.66g; Fiber 5.2g; Sugar 4.04g; Protein 1.95g

Pickled Red Onions

Prep Time: 3 minutes | Cook Time: 0 minute | Serves: 3

1 red onion, thinly sliced

1 cup cider vinegar

1 tablespoon whole black peppercorns (optional)

1. In a small bowl, combine the red onion with the cider vinegar and black peppercorns. Allow the onions to marinate for at least 15 minutes and up to 1 hour at room temperature. 2. Serve immediately or store in the refrigerator in an airtight container for up to 1 week.

Per Serving: Calories 37; Fat 0.11g; Sodium 6mg; Carbs 5.64g; Fiber 1.2g; Sugar 1.89g; Protein 0.64g

Smoky Deviled Eggs

Prep Time: 10 minutes | Cook Time: 15 minutes | Serves: 6

6 large eggs

3 tablespoons mayonnaise

1 teaspoon Dijon mustard

1 teaspoon hot sauce (such as Tabasco or Crystal)

¾ teaspoon smoked paprika (sweet or hot), plus more for serving

1 tablespoon chopped fresh chives

1. Add 1 cup water into the Instant Pot and place the wire metal steam rack or an egg rack into the pot. Gently arrange the eggs on the rack, being careful not to break the eggs when adding them. 2. Secure the lid and set the Pressure Release to Sealing. Select the Steam or Egg setting and set the cooking time for 5 minutes at high pressure. (The pot will take approximately 10 minutes to come up to pressure before the cooking program begins.) 3. While the eggs are cooking, prepare an ice bath. 4. When the cooking program ends, let the pressure release naturally for 5 minutes, then move the Pressure Release to Venting to release any remaining steam. Open the pot and transfer the eggs to the ice bath to cool for about 10 minutes. 5. Roll each egg around on the countertop to crack the entire shell and loosen the membrane, then, starting at the pointy end of the egg, peel off the shell. Slice the eggs in half lengthwise and transfer the yolks to a medium bowl. Arrange the egg white halves, hollow-side up, on a work surface.

6. Using a fork, mash the yolks thoroughly. Add the mayonnaise, hot sauce, mustard, and paprika and stir until the ingredients are evenly combined and the filling is smooth. Spoon or pipe the filling into the egg white halves. (At this point, you can store them in an airtight container in the refrigerator for up to 1 day.) 7. Sprinkle the deviled eggs with the chives and additional paprika before serving.

Per Serving: Calories 89; Fat 6.17g; Sodium 94mg; Carbs 1.76g; Fiber 0.2g; Sugar 0.56g; Protein 6.4g

Chapter 4 Poultry Mains

Garlicky Rosemary Chicken Thighs

Prep Time: 20 minutes | Cook Time: 20 minutes | Serves: 4-6

5 tablespoons extra-virgin olive oil, divided

3 medium shallots, diced

4 garlic cloves, peeled and crushed

1 rosemary sprig

2 to 2½ pounds bone-in, skin-on chicken thighs (about 6

pieces)

2 teaspoons kosher salt

¼ teaspoon freshly ground black pepper

1 lemon, juiced and zested

⅓ cup low-sodium chicken broth

1. In a large sauté pan or skillet, heat 3 tablespoons of olive oil over medium heat. Add the shallots and garlic and cook for about a minute, until fragrant. Add the rosemary sprig. 2. Season the chicken with the pepper and salt. Place the chicken in the skillet, skin-side down, and brown for 3 to 5 minutes. 3. Once it's cooked halfway through, turn the chicken over and add lemon juice and zest. 4. Add the chicken broth, cover the pan, and continue cooking for 10 to 15 more minutes, until cooked through and juices run clear. 5. Serve and enjoy.

Per Serving: Calories 392; Fat 28.12g; Sodium 879mg; Carbs 2.33g; Fiber 0.3g; Sugar 0.63g; Protein 31.21g

Lemony Chicken Kebabs

Prep Time: 45 minutes | Cook Time: 20 minutes | Serves: 4

½ cup extra-virgin olive oil, divided

½ large lemon, juiced

2 garlic cloves, minced

½ teaspoon za'atar seasoning

Salt

Freshly ground black pepper

1 pound boneless skinless chicken breasts, cut into 1¼-inch cubes

1 large red bell pepper, cut into 1¼-inch pieces

2 small zucchini (nearly 1 pound), cut into rounds slightly under ½ inch thick

2 large shallots, diced into quarters

1. In a bowl, whisk together ⅓ cup of olive oil, garlic, za'atar, salt, lemon juice, and pepper. 2. Put the chicken in a medium bowl and pour the olive oil mixture over the chicken. Press the chicken into the marinade. Cover and refrigerate for 45 minutes. While the chicken marinates, soak the wooden skewers in water for 30 minutes. 3. Drizzle and toss the pepper, zucchini, and shallots with the remaining 2½ tablespoons of olive oil and season lightly with the salt. 4. Preheat the oven to 500°F and place a baking sheet in the oven to heat. 5. On each skewer, thread a red bell pepper, zucchini, shallot and 2 chicken pieces and repeat twice. Put the kebabs onto the hot baking sheet and cook for 7 to 9 minutes, or until the chicken is cooked through. Rotate once halfway through cooking. 6. Serve the kebabs warm.

Per Serving: Calories 412; Fat 30.48g; Sodium 373mg; Carbs 6.74g; Fiber 1.7g; Sugar 1.17g; Protein 29.1g

Grilled Chicken Kebabs with Zucchini and Olives

Nonstick cooking spray

¼ cup extra-virgin olive oil

2 tablespoons balsamic vinegar

1 teaspoon dried oregano, crushed between your fingers

1 pound boneless, skinless chicken breasts, cut into 1½-inch

pieces

2 medium zucchini, cut into 1-inch pieces (about 2½ cups)

½ cup Kalamata olives, pitted and halved

2 tablespoons olive brine

¼ cup torn fresh basil leaves

1. Coat the cold grill with nonstick cooking spray. Heat the grill to medium-high. 2. In a small bowl, whisk together the oil, vinegar, and oregano. Divide the marinade between two large plastic zip-top bags. 3. Add the chicken to one bag and the zucchini to another. Seal and massage the marinade into both the chicken and zucchini. 4. Thread the chicken onto 6 (12-inch) wooden skewers. Thread the zucchini onto 8 or 9 (12-inch) wooden skewers. Cook the kebabs in batches on the grill for 5 minutes, flip, and grill for another 5 minutes, until any chicken juices run clear. 5. Remove the chicken and zucchini from the skewers and put in a large serving bowl. Toss with the olives, olive brine, and basil and serve.

Per Serving: Calories 338; Fat 20.14g; Sodium 533mg; Carbs 6.4g; Fiber 2g; Sugar 1.21g; Protein 35.16g

Lemon-Garlic Chicken

¼ cup freshly squeezed lemon juice

4 tablespoons olive oil, divided

6 garlic cloves, minced

1 tablespoon chopped fresh oregano

1 teaspoon ground cumin

1 teaspoon ground coriander

1 pound boneless, skinless chicken breast tenders

Sea salt

Freshly ground black pepper

1 onion, sliced

2 lemons, cut into wedges

Chopped fresh parsley, for garnish

1. In a medium bowl, add the lemon juice, 2 tablespoons of olive oil, garlic, oregano, cumin, and coriander and mix well. 2. Season the chicken with the pepper and salt and place the chicken and the onion in the marinade. Toss to coat. Cover and let rest for at least 20 minutes or refrigerate for up to 8 hours. 3. In a large cast iron skillet, heat the remaining 2 tablespoons of olive oil over medium heat. 4. Add the chicken tenders to the skillet in a single layer, discarding any marinade left behind. 5. Cook on each side for 6 to 7 minutes, flipping once, until browned and the juices run clear. 6. Transfer the chicken and onions to a serving platter. Serve with the lemon wedges and garnish with the parsley.

Per Serving: Calories 314; Fat 17.92g; Sodium 667mg; Carbs 7.7g; Fiber 1.2g; Sugar 2.24g; Protein 32.77g

Pineapple-Orange Grilled Chicken Breasts

Prep Time: 10 minutes | Cook Time: 7-10 minutes | Serves: 4

6 ounces pineapple juice

4 ounces orange juice

¼ cup cider vinegar

1 tablespoon fresh tarragon, chopped

½ tablespoon fresh rosemary

1 pound boneless chicken breast, skinned and cut into 4 pieces

1. About 3 to 4 hours before you are ready to grill, make the marinade: In a large shallow dish, combine the pineapple juice, orange juice, vinegar, tarragon, and rosemary. 2. Place the raw chicken breasts into the marinade. Cover and refrigerate for 3 to 4 hours. Turn pieces of chicken over during marinade process to cover with marinade. 3. Heat the grill to medium-high. 4. Place the chicken on the grill. Grill for approximately 7 to 10 minutes on each side, until chicken is cooked through. 5. Serve and enjoy.

Per Serving: Calories 235; Fat 10.64g; Sodium 74mg; Carbs 8.83g; Fiber 0.2g; Sugar 6.69g; Protein 24.11g

Parsley Chicken and Potatoes

Prep Time: 15 minutes | Cook Time: 25 minutes | Serves: 6

1½ pounds boneless, skinless chicken thighs, cut into 1-inch cubes

1 tablespoon extra-virgin olive oil

1½ pounds Yukon Gold potatoes, unpeeled, cut into ½-inch cubes (about 6 small potatoes)

2 garlic cloves, minced (about 1 teaspoon)

¼ cup apple cider vinegar

1 cup low-sodium or no-salt-added chicken broth

1 tablespoon Dijon mustard

¼ teaspoon kosher or sea salt

¼ teaspoon freshly ground black pepper

1 cup chopped fresh flat-leaf (Italian) parsley, including stems

1 tablespoon freshly squeezed lemon juice (½ small lemon)

1. Pat the chicken dry with a few paper towels. In a large skillet, heat the oil over medium-high heat. Add the chicken and cook for 5 minutes, stirring only after the chicken has browned on one side. Remove the chicken from the pan with a slotted spoon and put on a plate; it will not yet be fully cooked. Leave the skillet on the stove. 2. Add the potatoes to the skillet and cook for 5 minutes, stirring only after the potatoes have become golden and crispy on one side. Push the potatoes to the side of the skillet, add the garlic, and cook, stirring constantly, for 1 minute. Add the vinegar and cook for 1 minute, until nearly evaporated. Add the chicken broth, mustard, pepper, salt, and reserved chicken pieces. Turn the heat up to high, and bring to a boil. 3. Once boiling, cover the skillet, reduce the heat to medium-low, and cook for 10 to 12 minutes, until the potatoes are tender and the internal temperature of the chicken measures 165°F on a meat thermometer and any juices run clear. 4. During the last minute of cooking, stir in the parsley. Remove from the heat, stir in the lemon juice, and serve.

Per Serving: Calories 390; Fat 16.22g; Sodium 635mg; Carbs 31.6g; Fiber 3.3g; Sugar 2.31g; Protein 29.54g

Tunisian Herb Chicken Skewers

¼ cup olive oil

¼ cup freshly squeezed lemon juice

1 tablespoon chopped fresh thyme

2 tablespoons smoked paprika

1 tablespoon minced garlic

1 tablespoon chopped fresh parsley

1 teaspoon ground cumin

1 pound boneless, skinless chicken breasts, cut into 1½-inch chunks

1. In a large bowl, stir together the olive oil, lemon juice, thyme, paprika, garlic, parsley, and cumin until well mixed. Add the chicken, stirring to coat, cover, and refrigerate 2 hours. 2. Preheat a grill to medium high. Soak 8 bamboo skewers in warm water. 3. Thread the chicken chunks onto the soaked wooden skewers. Grill until the chicken is browned and cooked through, turning occasionally, 8 to 10 minutes. 4. Serve.

Per Serving: Calories 269; Fat 17.36g; Sodium 302mg; Carbs 4.03g; Fiber 1.4g; Sugar 0.78g; Protein 26.26g

Lemon Chicken and Roasted Artichokes

2 large lemons

3 tablespoons extra-virgin olive oil, divided

½ teaspoon kosher or sea salt

2 large artichokes

4 (6-ounce) bone-in, skin-on chicken thighs

1. Put a large, rimmed baking sheet in the oven. Preheat the oven to 450°F with the pan inside. Tear off four sheets of aluminum foil about 8-by-10 inches each and set aside. 2. Using a Microplane or citrus zester, zest 1 lemon into a large bowl. Halve both lemons and squeeze all the juice into the bowl with the zest. Whisk in 2 tablespoons of oil and the salt. Set aside. 3. Rinse the artichokes with cool water and dry with a clean towel. Using a sharp knife, cut about 1½ inches off the tip of each artichoke. Cut about ¼ inch off each stem. Halve each artichoke lengthwise so each piece has equal amounts of stem. Immediately plunge the artichoke halves into the lemon juice and oil mixture (to prevent browning) and turn to coat on all sides. Lay one artichoke half flat-side down in the center of a sheet of aluminum foil, and close up loosely to make a foil packet. Repeat the process with the remaining three artichoke halves. Set the packets aside. 4. Put the chicken in the remaining lemon juice mixture and turn to coat. 5. Using oven mitts, carefully remove the hot baking sheet from the oven, pour on the remaining tablespoon of oil, and tilt the pan to coat. Carefully arrange the chicken, skin-side down, on the hot baking sheet. Place the artichoke packets, flat-side down, on the baking sheet as well. (Arrange the artichoke packets and chicken with space between them so air can circulate around them.) 6. Roast for 20 minutes, or until the internal temperature of the chicken measures 165°F on a meat thermometer and any juices run clear. Before serving, check the artichokes for doneness by pulling on a leaf. If it comes out easily, the artichoke is ready.

Per Serving: Calories 509; Fat 38.56g; Sodium 505mg; Carbs 10.59g; Fiber 4.4g; Sugar 1.41g; Protein 30.83g

Moroccan Chicken with Sweet Potato Hash

Prep Time: 15 minutes | Cook Time: 40 minutes | Serves: 4

¼ teaspoon ground cumin

¼ teaspoon ground coriander

¼ teaspoon ground ginger

¼ teaspoon ground cinnamon

4 (3-ounce) boneless, skinless chicken breasts

2 tablespoons olive oil, divided

1 pound sweet potatoes, peeled and cut into ½-inch cubes

1 red bell pepper, chopped

1 zucchini, chopped

½ sweet onion, chopped

2 teaspoons minced garlic

2 cups stemmed, chopped kale

Sea salt

Freshly ground black pepper

1. In a small bowl, stir together the cumin, coriander, ginger, and cinnamon. Dredge the chicken breasts in the spices so they are well coated. 2. In a large skillet, heat 1 tablespoon of olive oil over medium-high heat. Pan-fry the chicken until completely cooked through, turning once, about 15 minutes total. 3. Transfer the chicken to a plate and cover with aluminum foil to keep warm. 4. Add the remaining 1 tablespoon of olive oil to the skillet and sauté the sweet potatoes until tender, about 15 minutes. 5. Add the bell pepper, zucchini, onion, and garlic and sauté until the vegetables are softened and heated through, stirring occasionally, about 5 minutes. 6. Add the kale and sauté until wilted, about 4 minutes more. Season with the salt and pepper. Evenly divide between plates, top each with a chicken breast, and serve.

Per Serving: Calories 330; Fat 10.54g; Sodium 652mg; Carbs 32.63g; Fiber 6.1g; Sugar 8.2g; Protein 29.32g

North African Chicken Apricot Tagine

Prep Time: 10 minutes | Cook Time: 50 minutes | Serves: 4

2 tablespoons olive oil, divided

1 pound boneless skinless chicken breast, cut into 1-inch chunks

½ sweet onion, chopped

1 tablespoon minced garlic

2 teaspoons peeled grated fresh ginger

2 cups cauliflower florets

2 carrots, cut in half lengthwise and sliced

1 (15-ounce) can low-sodium diced tomatoes

¼ cup chopped dried apricots

1 teaspoon ground cumin

½ teaspoon ground cinnamon

Sea salt

1. Preheat the oven to 400°F. 2. In a large ovenproof skillet, heat 1 tablespoon of olive oil. Brown the chicken until golden, about 10 minutes total. Transfer to a plate and set aside. 3. Add the remaining 1 tablespoon of olive oil and sauté the onion, garlic, and ginger until softened, about 3 minutes. Add the cauliflower and carrots and sauté for 5 minutes more. 4. Stir in the chicken, tomatoes and their juices, apricots, cumin, and cinnamon. Cover and braise in the oven until the vegetables are tender and the chicken is cooked through, 20 to 25 minutes. Season with the salt and serve.

Per Serving: Calories 273; Fat 10.19g; Sodium 439mg; Carbs 17.27g; Fiber 3.2g; Sugar 11.61g; Protein 28.06g

Pan-Fried Chicken Breasts with Roasted Squash Salsa

Prep Time: 15 minutes | Cook Time: 20 minutes | Serves: 4

½ butternut squash, peeled and cut into ¼-inch cubes

1 tablespoon olive oil, divided

1 teaspoon ground cinnamon

Sea salt

Freshly ground black pepper

1 pear, cored and chopped

1 scallion, both white and green parts, thinly sliced on the bias

1 tablespoon freshly squeezed lemon juice

4 (3-ounce) boneless, skinless chicken breasts, pounded to 1-inch thick

1. Preheat the oven to 400°F. Line a baking sheet with aluminum foil and set aside. 2. In a medium bowl, toss the squash with 1 teaspoon of olive oil and the cinnamon. Season the squash lightly with the salt and pepper. 3. Spread the squash on the baking sheet and bake until tender and lightly caramelized, about 15 minutes. Transfer from the baking sheet to a medium bowl and let cool for about 10 minutes. 4. Stir in the pear, scallion, and lemon juice, toss to combine, and set aside. 5. While the squash is baking, in a large skillet, heat the remaining 2 teaspoons of olive oil over medium-high heat. 6. Season the chicken breast with the salt and pepper and pan-fry until golden and cooked through, turning once, about 15 minutes. 7. Serve the chicken with the roasted squash salsa.

Per Serving: Calories 194; Fat 10.43g; Sodium 345mg; Carbs 11.17g; Fiber 2.8g; Sugar 3.6g; Protein 15.69g

Chicken Lentil Bowl with Roasted Red Pepper Dressing

Prep Time: 25 minutes | Cook Time: 0 minute | Serves: 4

For the Dressing:

½ cup store-bought or homemade roasted red peppers

¼ cup olive oil

2 tablespoons balsamic vinegar

For the Lentil Bowl:

2 (15-ounce) cans low-sodium lentils

2 cups chopped store-bought rotisserie chicken

2 cups halved cherry tomatoes

½ English cucumber, chopped

½ teaspoon minced garlic

Sea salt

Freshly ground black pepper

1 cup shredded kale

1 cup chopped marinated artichoke hearts

2 tablespoons chopped fresh basil

To make the dressing: 1. In a blender, combine the roasted red peppers, olive oil, balsamic vinegar, and garlic and pulse until finely chopped and smooth. Season with the pepper and salt and set aside.

To make the lentil bowl: 1. In a large bowl, toss together the lentils, chicken, and cherry tomatoes until mixed. 2. Divide the lentil mixture between the bowls and top them evenly with the cucumber, kale, artichoke hearts, and basil. Drizzle the roasted red pepper dressing over the bowls and serve.

Per Serving: Calories 661; Fat 21.52g; Sodium 442mg; Carbs 78.77g; Fiber 15.2g; Sugar 7.37g; Protein 42.94g

Turkey with Spinach and Spinach

Prep Time: 15 minutes | Cook Time: 30 minutes | Serves: 4

1 tablespoon olive oil

1 pound lean ground turkey

1 sweet onion, chopped

2 celery stalks, chopped

2 carrots, peeled and chopped

1 tablespoon minced garlic

2 cups low-sodium chicken stock

2 large tomatoes, chopped

1 (15-ounce) can low-sodium chickpeas, drained and rinsed

1 tablespoon sweet paprika

Dash cayenne pepper

3 cups chopped spinach

Juice of 1 lemon

¼ cup chopped fresh cilantro

Sea salt

Freshly ground black pepper

1. In a large saucepan, heat the olive oil over medium-high heat and brown the ground turkey until cooked through, about 7 minutes. 2. Stir in the onion, celery, carrots, and garlic and sauté for 4 minutes. 3. Stir in the chicken stock, tomatoes, chickpeas, paprika, and cayenne and bring the stew to a boil. Reduce the heat to low and simmer until the vegetables are tender, about 15 minutes. 4. Stir in the spinach, lemon juice, and cilantro and season with the pepper and salt. Let stand for 5 minutes to wilt the spinach and serve.

Per Serving: Calories 387; Fat 16.34g; Sodium 604mg; Carbs 32.31g; Fiber 8.8g; Sugar 11.63g; Protein 31.8g

Lemon Garlic Chicken Breasts

Prep Time: 25 minutes | Cook Time: 2½–5½ hours | Serves: 6

1 tsp. dried oregano

½ tsp. seasoned salt

¼ tsp. pepper

6 (5 oz. each) chicken-breast halves, skinned and rinsed

2 Tbsp. canola oil

¼ cup water

3 Tbsp. lemon juice

2 garlic cloves, minced

1 tsp. chicken bouillon granules

1 Tbsp. minced fresh parsley

1. Combine the oregano, salt, and pepper. Rub all of mixture into the chicken. Brown the chicken in the canola oil in the skillet. Transfer to the slow cooker. 2. Place the water, lemon juice, garlic, and bouillon cubes in skillet. Bring to a boil, loosening the browned bits from the skillet. Pour over the chicken. 3. Cover. Cook on high for 2 to 2½ hours, or low for 4 to 5 hours. 4. Add the parsley and baste the chicken. Cover. Cook on high for 15 to 30 minutes, until the chicken is tender.

Per Serving: Calories 251; Fat 9.83g; Sodium 664mg; Carbs 1.36g; Fiber 0.2g; Sugar 0.28g; Protein 39.95g

Chicken Breasts with Onions

Prep Time: 10 minutes | Cook Time: 4 hours | Serves: 7

1 medium onion, sliced

2½-lb. boneless, skinless chicken breasts

½ tsp. seasoned salt

¼ tsp. pepper

½ tsp. garlic powder

1. Layer the onion in the bottom of slow cooker. Add the chicken and sprinkle with the pepper, seasoned salt, and garlic powder. 2. Cook on low for 4 hours or until done but not dry. 3. Serve and enjoy.

Per Serving: Calories 241; Fat 5.8g; Sodium 698mg; Carbs 1.79g; Fiber 0.3g; Sugar 0.75g; Protein 45.67g

Turkish Chicken Kebabs

Prep Time: 40 minutes | Cook Time: 20 minutes | Serves: 4-6

2 white onions, chopped

2 garlic cloves, crushed

¾ cup extra-virgin olive oil, divided

2 tablespoons lemon juice

1 teaspoon dried oregano

2 teaspoons salt, divided

½ teaspoon curry powder

½ teaspoon ground turmeric

1½ pounds boneless chicken breast or thigh meat, cut into 1-inch pieces

12 skewers

2 red onions, cut into 1-inch pieces

3 to 4 zucchini, cut into 1-inch rounds

¼ teaspoon freshly ground black pepper

½ lemon

1 tablespoon chopped fresh mint

1. Place the onions, garlic, ½ cup olive oil, lemon juice, oregano, 1 teaspoon salt, curry powder, and turmeric in a blender or food processor and process until puréed. 2. Add the chicken in a medium bowl, pour the marinade over, cover, and marinate in the refrigerator for at least 30 minutes, or overnight. 3. Thread the skewers by beginning with a piece of red onion, a piece of chicken, a piece of zucchini, a piece of chicken, and another piece of red onion. Place the skewers on a baking sheet. 4. When all the skewers have been made, brush with the remaining ¼ cup olive oil and sprinkle with 1 teaspoon salt and the pepper. 5. Heat a grill or broiler until hot. Cook the skewers over a hot grill or in a broiler until the meat is cooked, about 6 to 8 minutes per side. 6. Season the cooked kebabs with freshly squeezed lemon juice and garnish with chopped mint. 7. Let the kebabs sit for about 5 minutes before serving. 8. After the meat has marinated, the skewers can be made and kept in the refrigerator for several hours before grilling. Once cooked, the chicken can be stored in the refrigerator for about 1 week.

Per Serving: Calories 434; Fat 30.57g; Sodium 834mg; Carbs 11.86g; Fiber 2.9g; Sugar 3.37g; Protein 29.6g

Traditional Chicken Kalamata

Prep Time: 15 minutes | Cook Time: 40 minutes | Serves: 4

2 tablespoons olive oil

1 cup chopped onion

1 teaspoon minced garlic

1½ cups chopped green peppers

1 pound boneless, skinless chicken breast, cut into 4 pieces

2 cups diced tomatoes

1 teaspoon oregano

½ cup pitted, chopped Kalamata olives

1. In a large skillet, heat the olive oil over medium heat. Add the onions, garlic, and peppers and sauté for about 5 minutes until the onions are translucent. 2. Add the chicken pieces. Cook for about 5 minutes each side until lightly brown. 3. Add the tomatoes and oregano. Reduce the heat and simmer for 20 minutes. 4. Add the olives and simmer for another 10 minutes before serving.

Per Serving: Calories 277; Fat 12.66g; Sodium 503mg; Carbs 9.21g; Fiber 2.4g; Sugar 4.46g; Protein 33.46g

Chicken Thighs with Chilli Sauce

Prep Time: 15 minutes | Cook Time: 20-25 minutes | Serves: 6

2 tablespoons extra virgin olive oil

3 rosemary sprigs, halved

12 boneless and skinless chicken thighs

2 onions, cut into 8 wedges

2 red bell or Romano peppers

2 courgettes or 1 aubergine or 1 small head of broccoli

2 handfuls of watercress, rocket or lettuce

Salt and freshly ground black pepper

1 lemon, cut into wedges, to serve

For the Chilli Sauce:

1–2 red chillies, depending on strength, or ⅓ teaspoon chilli flakes

2 garlic cloves

6 tablespoons olive oil

1 sprig of rosemary, stem discarded

¼ teaspoon salt and plenty of freshly ground black pepper

1. Preheat the oven to 220°C/200°C fan/475°F/gas mark 7. 2. Lightly oil a baking tray with 1 teaspoon of the oil and scatter over the rosemary. Season the chicken thighs on both sides and lay them over the rosemary, stretching them out flat so that they cook quickly. Scatter the onions, peppers and courgettes around the edges of the chicken, season and drizzle with the remaining oil. Cook for 20 to 25 minutes until the chicken thighs are cooked through. There should be no pink juices when you pierce the thickest part of the thigh or the internal temperature should be higher than 74°C (165°F). 3. Meanwhile, make the sauce. Taste a red pepper from where the pith meets the seeds in the center of the pepper to see how spicy it is and then decide whether to use one or two. If neither are spicy enough, add a pinch of chilli flakes. Put all the sauce ingredients in a small food processor and whizz to combine or chop finely by hand and mix together. Transfer to a jug and set aside. 4. Divide the cooked chicken and vegetables between 6 plates. Add a little watercress and a lemon wedge to each plate and serve with the sauce on the side.

Per Serving: Calories 408; Fat 22.23g; Sodium 297mg; Carbs 18.04g; Fiber 4.3g; Sugar 9.37g; Protein 35.43g

Best Roast Chicken

Prep Time: 15 minutes | Cook Time: 4-10 hours | Serves: 6

3-lb. whole frying chicken

Half an onion, chopped

1 rib celery, chopped

Salt to taste

Pepper to taste

½ tsp. poultry seasoning

¼ tsp. dried basil

1. Sprinkle the chicken cavity with the salt, pepper, and poultry seasoning. Put the onion and celery inside cavity. Put the chicken in the slow cooker and sprinkle with the basil. 2. Cover. Cook on low for 8 to 10 hours, or high 4 to 6 hours. 3. Remove the skin from the chicken and discard the liquid. 4. Serve and enjoy.

Per Serving: Calories 509; Fat 20.75g; Sodium 416mg; Carbs 6.65g; Fiber 0.8g; Sugar 1.61g; Protein 69.71g

Italian Chicken and Sausage Cacciatore

Prep Time: 30 minutes | Cook Time: 8 hours | Serves: 6

1 large green pepper, sliced in 1" strips

1 cup sliced mushrooms

1 medium onion, sliced in rings

1 lb. skinless, boneless chicken breasts, browned

1 lb. lean sweet Italian turkey sausage, browned

½ tsp. dried oregano

½ tsp. dried basil

2 Tbsp. Italian seasoning mix

1½ cups no-added-salt tomato sauce

1. Layer the vegetables in the slow cooker. 2. Top with the meat. 3. Sprinkle with the oregano, basil, and Italian seasoning mix. 4. Top with the tomato sauce. 5. Cover. Cook on low 8 hours. 6. Remove the cover during last 30 minutes of cooking time to allow the sauce to cook-off and thicken.

Per Serving: Calories 268; Fat 9.08g; Sodium 680mg; Carbs 9.38g; Fiber 1.9g; Sugar 3.88g; Protein 38.03g

Slow Cooker Turkey Breast

Prep Time: 15 minutes | Cook Time: 9-10 hours | Serves: 12

6-lb. turkey breast, skin and visible fat removed

2 tsp. oil

Salt and pepper to taste

1 onion, quartered

4 garlic cloves, peeled

½ cup water

1. Rinse the turkey and pat dry with paper towels. 2. Rub the oil over the turkey. Sprinkle with the salt and pepper. Place, meaty side up, in a large slow cooker. 3. Place the onion and garlic around sides of the cooker. 4. Cover. Cook on low 9-10 hours, or until the meat thermometer stuck in meaty part of breast registers 170°F. 5. Remove from the slow cooker and let stand 10 minutes before slicing.

Per Serving: Calories 298; Fat 8.62g; Sodium 582mg; Carbs 1.31g; Fiber 0.2g; Sugar 0.4g; Protein 50.44g

Garlicky Turkey Breast with Orange Sauce

Prep Time: 15 minutes | Cook Time: 7-8 hours | Serves: 6

1 large onion, chopped

3 garlic cloves, minced

1 tsp. dried rosemary

½ tsp. pepper

2-lb. boneless, skinless turkey breast

1½ cups orange juice

1. Place the onions in slow cooker. 2. Combine the garlic, rosemary, and pepper. 3. Make the gashes in the turkey, about ¾ of the way through at 2" intervals. Stuff with the herb mixture. Place the turkey in the slow cooker. 4. Pour the juice over the turkey. 5. Cover. Cook on low for 7 to 8 hours, or until the turkey is no longer pink in center.

Per Serving: Calories 194; Fat 2.68g; Sodium 313mg; Carbs 9.64g; Fiber 0.6g; Sugar 6.36g; Protein 33.4g

Turkey Cacciatore

Prep Time: 15 minutes | Cook Time: 4 hours | Serves: 6

2½ cups chopped cooked turkey

¾ tsp. salt

Dash pepper

1 Tbsp. dried onion flakes

1 green pepper, minced

1 clove garlic, minced

15-oz. can whole tomatoes, mashed

4-oz. can sliced mushrooms, drained

2 tsp. tomato paste

1 bay leaf

¼ tsp. dried thyme

2 Tbsp. finely chopped pimento

1. Combine all ingredients well in the slow cooker. 2. Cover. Cook on low 4 hours. 3. Serve and enjoy.

Per Serving: Calories 179; Fat 8.17g; Sodium 435mg; Carbs 5.5g; Fiber 2.1g; Sugar 3.31g; Protein 22.25g

Chapter 5 Fish and Seafood Mains

Seared Sea Scallops with Spring Vegetables

Prep Time: 5 minutes | Cook Time: 12 minutes | Serves: 4

2 tablespoons extra-virgin olive oil, divided

12 large sea scallops (about 1 pound), side muscles removed, patted dry

⅛ teaspoon freshly ground black pepper

8 ounces asparagus, ends trimmed

1 cup snap peas

1 cup baby carrots, halved lengthwise

1 medium shallot, finely chopped

2 garlic cloves, minced

¼ cup reduced-sodium vegetable stock

6 ounces baby spinach

1. In a large skillet, heat 1 tablespoon of olive oil over medium-high heat. Sprinkle the scallops with the black pepper and add them to the skillet. Cook for about 2 minutes per side, or until just golden. Transfer to a plate and cover the plate loosely with aluminum foil to keep them warm. 2. Add the remaining 1 tablespoon of olive oil to the skillet, along with the asparagus, snap peas, carrots, shallot, and garlic. Cook for about 4 minutes, stirring often, or until the vegetables are tender-crisp. Add the vegetable stock and spinach and continue to cook for 1 to 2 minutes, or until the spinach is slightly wilted. 3. Serve the vegetables alongside the scallops. 4. Refrigerate the leftovers in an airtight container for up to 5 days.

Per Serving: Calories 205; Fat 7.77g; Sodium 505mg; Carbs 16.48g; Fiber 5g; Sugar 4.96g; Protein 18.57g

Salmon with Tomatoes and Red Peppers

Prep Time: 15 minutes | Cook Time: 15 minutes | Serves: 4

1 tablespoon extra-virgin olive oil

2 garlic cloves, minced (about 1 teaspoon)

1 teaspoon smoked paprika

1 pint grape or cherry tomatoes, quartered (about 1½ cups)

1 (12-ounce) jar roasted red peppers, drained and chopped

1 tablespoon water

¼ teaspoon freshly ground black pepper

¼ teaspoon kosher or sea salt

1 pound salmon fillets, skin removed, cut into 8 pieces

1 tablespoon freshly squeezed lemon juice (from ½ medium lemon)

1. In a large skillet, heat the oil over medium heat. Add the garlic and smoked paprika and cook for 1 minute, stirring often. Add the tomatoes, roasted peppers, water, black pepper, and salt. Turn up the heat to medium-high, bring to a simmer, and cook for 3 minutes, stirring occasionally and smashing the tomatoes with a wooden spoon toward the end of the cooking time. 2. Add the salmon to the skillet and spoon some of the sauce over the top. Cover and cook for 10 to 12 minutes, or until the salmon is cooked through (145°F using a meat thermometer) and just starts to flake. 3. Remove the skillet from the heat and drizzle lemon juice over the top of the fish. Stir the sauce, then break up the salmon into chunks with a fork. Serve and enjoy.

Per Serving: Calories 203; Fat 8.03g; Sodium 408mg; Carbs 8.54g; Fiber 2g; Sugar 5.38g; Protein 24.32g

Tilapia with Red Onion and Avocado

Prep Time: 10 minutes | Cook Time: 5 minutes | Serves: 4

1 tablespoon extra-virgin olive oil

1 tablespoon freshly squeezed orange juice

¼ teaspoon kosher or sea salt

4 (4-ounce) tilapia fillets, more oblong than square, skin-on

or skinned

¼ cup chopped red onion (about ⅛ onion)

1 avocado, pitted, skinned, and sliced

1. In a 9-inch glass pie dish, mix together the oil, orange juice, and salt with a fork. Working with one fillet at a time, place each in the pie dish and turn to coat on all sides with the mixture. Arrange the fillets in a wagon-wheel formation so that one end of each fillet is in the center of the dish and the other end is temporarily draped over the edge of the dish. Place 1 tablespoon of onion on top of each fillet, then fold the fillet hanging over the edge over the onion. When finished, you should have 4 folded-over fillets with the fold against the outer edge of the dish and the ends all in the center. 2. Cover the dish with plastic wrap, leaving a small portion around the edges to allow steam to escape. Microwave on high for approximately 3 minutes. The fish is ready to serve when it starts to separate into flakes (chunks) when pressed gently with a fork. 3. Serve the fillets topped with avocado.

Per Serving: Calories 235; Fat 12.96g; Sodium 206mg; Carbs 7.02g; Fiber 4.4g; Sugar 2.47g; Protein 24.57g

Grilled Fish on Lemons

Prep Time: 10 minutes | Cook Time: 10 minutes | Serves: 4

4 (4-ounce) fish fillets, such as tilapia, salmon, catfish, cod,

or your favorite fish

Nonstick cooking spray

3 to 4 medium lemons

1 tablespoon extra-virgin olive oil

¼ teaspoon freshly ground black pepper

¼ teaspoon kosher or sea salt

1. Using paper towels, pat the fillets dry and let stand at room temperature for 10 minutes. Meanwhile, coat the cold cooking grate of the grill with nonstick cooking spray and preheat the grill to 400°F, or medium-high heat. Or preheat a grill pan over medium-high heat on the stove top. 2. Cut one lemon in half and set half aside. Slice the remaining half of that lemon and the remaining lemons into ¼-inch-thick slices. (You should have about 12 to 16 lemon slices.) Into a small bowl, squeeze 1 tablespoon of juice out of the reserved lemon half. 3. Add the oil to the bowl with the lemon juice and mix well. Brush both sides of the fish with the oil mixture and sprinkle evenly with the pepper and salt. 4. Carefully place the lemon slices on the grill (or the grill pan), arranging 3 to 4 slices together in the shape of a fish fillet, and repeat with the remaining slices. Place the fish fillets directly on top of the lemon slices, and grill with the lid closed. (If you're grilling on the stove top, cover with a large pot lid or aluminum foil.) Turn the fish halfway through the cooking time only if the fillets are more than half an inch thick. The fish is ready to serve when it starts to separate into flakes (chunks) when pressed gently with a fork.

Per Serving: Calories 242; Fat 15.35g; Sodium 199mg; Carbs 2.6g; Fiber 0.1g; Sugar 0.91g; Protein 22.74g

Fish Fillets with Green Beans and Tomatoes

Prep Time: 10 minutes | Cook Time: 10 minutes | Serves: 4

Nonstick cooking spray

2 tablespoons extra-virgin olive oil

1 tablespoon balsamic vinegar

4 (4-ounce) fish fillets, such as cod or tilapia (½ inch thick)

2½ cups green beans (about 12 ounces)

1 pint cherry or grape tomatoes (about 2 cups)

1. Preheat the oven to 400°F. Coat two large, rimmed baking sheets with nonstick cooking spray. 2. In a small bowl, whisk together the oil and vinegar. Set aside. 3. Place two pieces of fish on each baking sheet. 4. In a large bowl, combine the beans and tomatoes. Pour in the oil and vinegar, and toss gently to coat. Pour half of the green bean mixture over the fish on one baking sheet and the remaining half over the fish on the other. Turn the fish over and rub it in the oil mixture to coat. Spread the vegetables evenly on the baking sheets so hot air can circulate around them. 5. Bake for 5 to 8 minutes, until the fish is just opaque and not translucent. The fish is ready to serve when it starts to separate into flakes (chunks) when pressed gently with a fork.

Per Serving: Calories 182; Fat 7.61g; Sodium 354mg; Carbs 9.52g; Fiber 3.2g; Sugar 5.33g; Protein 19.55g

Orange-Garlic Shrimp

Prep Time: 20 minutes | Cook Time: 10 minutes | Serves: 6

1 large orange

3 tablespoons extra-virgin olive oil, divided

1 tablespoon chopped fresh rosemary (about 3 sprigs) or 1 teaspoon dried rosemary

1 tablespoon chopped fresh thyme (about 6 sprigs) or 1 teaspoon dried thyme

3 garlic cloves, minced (about 1½ teaspoons)

¼ teaspoon freshly ground black pepper

¼ teaspoon kosher or sea salt

1½ pounds fresh raw shrimp, (or frozen and thawed raw shrimp) shells and tails removed

1. Zest the entire orange using a Microplane or citrus grater. 2. In a large zip-top plastic bag, mix the orange zest, 2 tablespoons of oil, the rosemary, thyme, garlic, pepper, and salt. Add the shrimp, seal the bag, and gently massage the shrimp until all the ingredients are combined and the shrimp is completely covered with the seasonings. Set aside. 3. Heat a grill, grill pan, or a large skillet over medium heat. Brush on or swirl in the remaining 1 tablespoon of oil. Add half the shrimp and cook for 4 to 6 minutes, or until the shrimp turn pink and white, flipping halfway through if on the grill or stirring every minute if in a pan. Transfer the shrimp to a large serving bowl. Repeat with the remaining shrimp and add them to the bowl. 4. While the shrimp cook, peel the orange and cut the flesh into bite-size pieces. Add the orange to the serving bowl and toss with the cooked shrimp. Serve immediately or refrigerate and serve cold.

Per Serving: Calories 174; Fat 7.42g; Sodium 232mg; Carbs 4.44g; Fiber 1g; Sugar 2.89g; Protein 23.22g

Spicy Shrimp Puttanesca

2 tablespoons extra-virgin olive oil

3 anchovy fillets, drained and chopped (half a 2-ounce tin), or 1½ teaspoons anchovy paste

3 garlic cloves, minced (about 1½ teaspoons)

½ teaspoon crushed red pepper

1 (14.5-ounce) can low-sodium or no-salt-added diced tomatoes, undrained

1 (2.25-ounce) can sliced black olives, drained (about ½ cup)

2 tablespoons capers

1 tablespoon chopped fresh oregano or 1 teaspoon dried oregano

1 pound fresh raw shrimp (or frozen and thawed shrimp), shells and tails removed

1. In a large skillet, heat the oil over medium heat. Mix in the anchovies, garlic, and crushed red pepper. Cook for 3 minutes, stirring frequently and mashing up the anchovies with a wooden spoon, until they have melted into the oil. 2. Stir in the tomatoes with their juices, olives, capers, and oregano. Turn up the heat to medium-high and bring to a simmer. 3. When the sauce is lightly bubbling, stir in the shrimp. Reduce the heat to medium and cook for 6 to 8 minutes, or until the shrimps turn pink and white, stirring occasionally. 4. Serve.

Per Serving: Calories 214; Fat 9.89g; Sodium 379mg; Carbs 5.79g; Fiber 2.8g; Sugar 2.69g; Protein 26.92g

Trout with Ruby Red Grapefruit Relish

1 ruby red grapefruit, peeled, sectioned, and chopped

1 large navel orange, peeled, sectioned, and chopped

¼ English cucumber, chopped

2 tablespoons chopped red onion

1 tablespoon minced or grated lime zest

1 teaspoon minced fresh or canned peperoncino

1 teaspoon chopped fresh thyme

4 (4-ounce) trout fillets

Sea salt

Freshly ground black pepper

1 tablespoon olive oil

1. Preheat the oven to 400°F. 2. In a medium bowl, stir together the grapefruit, orange, cucumber, onion, lime zest, peperoncino, and thyme. Cover the relish with plastic wrap and set aside in the refrigerator. 3. Season the trout lightly with the pepper and salt and place on a baking sheet. 4. Brush the fish with the olive oil and roast in the oven until it flakes easily with a fork, about 15 minutes. 5. Serve topped with the chilled relish.

Per Serving: Calories 215; Fat 7.49g; Sodium 328mg; Carbs 12.71g; Fiber 2.1g; Sugar 9g; Protein 24.42g

Halibut with Kale and Cherry Tomatoes

Prep Time: 10 minutes | Cook Time: 15 minutes | Serves: 4

2 tablespoons olive oil, divided

3 cups coarsely chopped kale

2 cups halved cherry tomatoes

4 (4-ounce) boneless, skinless halibut fillets

Juice and zest of 1 lemon

Sea salt

Freshly ground black pepper

1 tablespoon chopped fresh basil

1. Preheat the oven to 375°F. Lightly grease an 8-by-8-inch baking dish with 2 teaspoons of olive oil. 2. Arrange the kale in the bottom of the baking dish and top with the cherry tomatoes and the halibut. Drizzle the remaining 1 tablespoon plus 1 teaspoon of olive oil and the lemon juice over the dish and season with the pepper and salt. Sprinkle with the lemon zest and basil. 3. Bake until the fish flakes easily and the greens are wilted, about 15 minutes. Serve.

Per Serving: Calories 312; Fat 23.1g; Sodium 405mg; Carbs 8.33g; Fiber 2.8g; Sugar 3.4g; Protein 19.2g

Crushed Marcona Almond Swordfish

Prep Time: 25 minutes | Cook Time: 15 minutes | Serves: 4

½ cup almond flour

¼ cup crushed Marcona almonds

½ to 1 teaspoon salt, divided

2 pounds Swordfish, preferably 1 inch thick

1 large egg, beaten (optional)

¼ cup pure apple cider

¼ cup extra-virgin olive oil, plus more for frying

3 to 4 sprigs flat-leaf parsley, chopped

1 lemon, juiced

1 tablespoon Spanish paprika

5 medium baby portobello mushrooms, chopped (optional)

4 or 5 chopped scallions, both green and white parts

3 to 4 garlic cloves, peeled

¼ cup chopped pitted Kalamata olives

1. On a dinner plate, spread the flour and crushed Marcona almonds and mix in the salt. Alternately, pour the flour, almonds, and ¼ teaspoon of salt into a large plastic food storage bag. Add the fish and coat it with the flour mixture. If a thicker coat is desired, repeat this step after dipping the fish in the egg (if using). 2. In a measuring cup, add the apple cider, ¼ cup of olive oil, parsley, lemon juice, paprika, and ¼ teaspoon of salt. Mix well and set aside. 3. In a large, heavy-bottom sauté pan or skillet, add the olive oil to a depth of ⅛ inch and heat on medium heat. When the oil is hot, add the fish and brown for 3 to 5 minutes, then turn the fish over and add the mushrooms (If using), scallions, garlic, and olives. Cook for an additional 3 minutes. Once the other side of the fish is brown, remove the fish from the pan and set aside. 4. Pour the cider mixture into the skillet and mix well with the vegetables. Put the fried fish into the skillet on top of the mixture and cook with the sauce on medium-low heat for 10 minutes, until the fish flakes easily with a fork. Remove the fish from the pan carefully and plate. Spoon the sauce over the fish. Serve with the home-fried potatoes.

Per Serving: Calories 590; Fat 34.65g; Sodium 564mg; Carbs 19.26g; Fiber 3.4g; Sugar 3.2g; Protein 50.13g

Trout with Roasted Red Pepper Sauce

Prep Time: 15 minutes | Cook Time: 6 minutes | Serves: 4

2 cups store-bought or homemade roasted red peppers

1 teaspoon minced garlic

Juice of 1 lemon

4 (4-ounce) trout fillets

Sea salt

Freshly ground black pepper

1 tablespoon olive oil

2 tablespoons chopped fresh parsley

1. In a blender, combine the roasted red peppers, lemon juice, and garlic and pulse until smooth. Set aside. 2. Lightly season the trout with the salt and pepper. 3. In a large skillet, heat the olive oil over medium-high heat. Cook the fillets for about 3 minutes, flip, and continue to cook until the fish is just cooked through and lightly golden, about 3 minutes. Serve topped with a generous spoonful of roasted red pepper sauce and a sprinkle of parsley.

Per Serving: Calories 194; Fat 7.54g; Sodium 546mg; Carbs 6.99g; Fiber 1.3g; Sugar 4.37g; Protein 24.24g

Simple Bouillabaisse

Prep Time: 10 minutes | Cook Time: 35 minutes | Serves: 4

1 tablespoon olive oil

½ sweet onion, chopped

3 celery stalks, chopped

1 cup chopped fennel

1 tablespoon minced garlic

4 cups fish stock or clam juice

2 tomatoes, chopped

1 tablespoon chopped fresh thyme

1 bay leaf

¼ teaspoon red pepper flakes

10 mussels, scrubbed and debearded

12 ounces boneless, skinless fish fillets, cut into 1-inch chunks (salmon, flounder, or halibut)

10 large shrimp, peeled and deveined

1 cup shredded kale

Sea salt

Freshly ground black pepper

1. In a large, deep skillet, heat the olive oil over medium-high heat. Sauté the onion, celery, fennel, and garlic until softened, about 6 minutes. 2. Add the fish stock, tomatoes, thyme, bay leaf, and red pepper flakes and bring to a boil. Reduce the heat to low and simmer for 10 minutes. 3. Add the mussels, cover the skillet, and simmer for 2 minutes more. 4. Add the fish and shrimp, cover, and simmer until the mussels open and the fish is just cooked through, 8 to 10 minutes. 5. Discard the bay leaf and add the kale to the skillet. Cover, remove from the heat, and let stand for 5 minutes so the kale wilts. 6. Season with pepper and salt and serve immediately.

Per Serving: Calories 234; Fat 7.37g; Sodium 1368mg; Carbs 11.67g; Fiber 2.4g; Sugar 5.07g; Protein 29.43g

Spicy Shrimp with Vegetables

Prep Time: 15 minutes | Cook Time: 12 minutes | Serves: 4

1 pound shrimp, peeled and deveined

3 baby bok choy, quartered

10 asparagus spears, trimmed and halved

1 yellow zucchini, sliced

1 red bell pepper, cut into thin strips

1 sweet onion, thinly sliced

1 tablespoon olive oil

½ teaspoon smoked paprika

½ teaspoon chili powder

½ teaspoon garlic powder

½ teaspoon ground cumin

Juice of 1 lime

1. Preheat the oven to 400°F. 2. In a large bowl, toss together the shrimp, bok choy, asparagus, zucchini, bell pepper, onion, olive oil, paprika, chili powder, garlic powder, and cumin until well coated. Spread the shrimp and vegetables on a baking sheet. 3. Bake until the shrimp are cooked through and vegetables are tender, stirring a few times, 10 to 12 minutes. Squeeze the lime juice over the shrimp and vegetables. 4. Serve.

Per Serving: Calories 207; Fat 4.6g; Sodium 173mg; Carbs 17.5g; Fiber 5g; Sugar 8.67g; Protein 27.5g

Whole Baked Trout with Lemon and Herbs

Prep Time: 10 minutes | Cook Time: 20 minutes | Serves: 4

1 tablespoon olive oil, divided

2 (8-ounce) whole trout, cleaned

Sea salt

Freshly ground black pepper

1 lemon, thinly sliced into about 6 pieces

1 tablespoon finely chopped fresh dill

1 tablespoon chopped fresh parsley

½ cup low-sodium fish stock or chicken stock

1. Preheat the oven to 400°F. 2. Lightly grease a 9-by-13-inch baking dish with 1 teaspoon of olive oil. 3. Rinse the trout, pat dry with paper towels, and coat with the remaining 2 teaspoons of olive oil. Season with the salt and pepper. 4. Stuff the interior of the trout with the lemon slices, dill, and parsley and place into the prepared baking dish. Bake the fish for 10 minutes and add the fish stock to the dish. 5. Continue to bake until the fish flakes easily with a fork, about 10 minutes. 6. Serve.

Per Serving: Calories 178; Fat 7.76g; Sodium 336mg; Carbs 2.35g; Fiber 0.5g; Sugar 0.35g; Protein 24.19g

Cod with Fresh Tomato Salsa

3 tomatoes, finely chopped

1 green bell pepper, finely chopped

¼ red onion, finely chopped

¼ cup pitted, chopped green olives

2 tablespoons white wine vinegar

1 tablespoon chopped fresh basil

½ teaspoon minced garlic

4 (4-ounce) cod fillets

Sea salt

Freshly ground black pepper

1 tablespoon olive oil

1. In a small bowl, stir together the tomatoes, bell pepper, onion, olives, vinegar, basil, and garlic until well mixed. Set aside. 2. Season the fish with the pepper and salt. 3. In a large skillet, heat the olive oil over medium-high heat. Pan-fry the fish, turning once, until it is just cooked through, about 4 minutes per side. 4. Transfer to the serving plates and top with a generous scoop of tomato salsa.

Per Serving: Calories 140; Fat 4.85g; Sodium 733mg; Carbs 5.21g; Fiber 1.4g; Sugar 0.87g; Protein 18.73g

Broiled Flounder with Nectarine and White Bean Salsa

2 nectarines, pitted and chopped

1 (15-ounce) can low-sodium cannellini beans, rinsed and drained

1 red bell pepper, chopped

1 scallion, both white and green parts, chopped

2 tablespoons chopped fresh cilantro

2 tablespoons freshly squeezed lime juice

4 (4-ounce) flounder fillets

1 teaspoon smoked paprika

Sea salt

Freshly ground black pepper

1. Preheat the oven to broil. 2. In a medium bowl, combine the nectarines, beans, bell pepper, scallion, cilantro, and lime juice. 3. Season the fish with the paprika, salt, and pepper. 4. Arrange the fish on a baking sheet and broil, turning once, until just cooked through, about 8 minutes total. 5. Serve the fish topped with the salsa.

Per Serving: Calories 228; Fat 3.73g; Sodium 1193mg; Carbs 26.03g; Fiber 6.7g; Sugar 7.56g; Protein 23.78g

Citrus Sea Scallops

Prep Time: 10 minutes | Cook Time: 4 minutes | Serves: 4

1 pound sea scallops

Sea salt

Freshly ground black pepper

2 tablespoons olive oil

Juice of 1 lime

Pinch red pepper flakes

1 tablespoon chopped fresh cilantro

1. Season the scallops lightly with the salt and pepper. 2. In a large skillet over medium-high heat, heat the olive oil. Add the scallops to the skillet, being carefully do not touch one another. 3. Sear on both sides, turning once, for a total of about 3 minutes. Add the red pepper flakes and lime juice to the skillet and toss the scallops in the juice. Serve topped with the cilantro.

Per Serving: Calories 146; Fat 7.35g; Sodium 289mg; Carbs 5.8g; Fiber 0.3g; Sugar 0.76g; Protein 13.98g

Roasted Salmon with Lemon and Dill

Prep Time: 10 minutes | Cook Time: 10-15 minutes | Serves: 4

1¼ pounds salmon, cut into 4 fillets

3 tablespoons lemon juice (from 1 large lemon)

2 tablespoons Dijon mustard

2 tablespoons chopped fresh dill

⅛ teaspoon ground black pepper

1. Preheat the oven to 450°F. Spray a medium baking pan with nonstick cooking spray. 2. Arrange the fillets in the baking pan. 3. In a small bowl, combine the remaining ingredients and brush tops and sides of the fillets with the mixture. Drizzle any remaining mixture over the fillets. 4. Place the pan on a middle rack in the oven and bake for 10 to 15 minutes, depending upon thickness of fillets. Fillets are done when they flake easily with a fork. 5. When done, remove from the oven and serve immediately.

Per Serving: Calories 192; Fat 6.59g; Sodium 599mg; Carbs 2.25g; Fiber 0.6g; Sugar 0.44g; Protein 29.73g

Grilled Tilapia with Peach-Mango Salsa

Prep Time: 10 minutes | Cook Time: 7-8 minutes | Serves: 4

2 tablespoons olive oil

2 tablespoons lime juice

¼ teaspoon salt

¼ teaspoon ground black pepper

1½ pounds tilapia fillets

1 cup Peach-Mango Salsa

1. In a medium shallow dish, mix the oil, lime juice, salt, and black pepper. Add the tilapia and turn to coat the fish with the marinade. 2. Heat the gas or charcoal grill or broiler to high. Coat a large piece of aluminum foil with nonstick cooking spray. Place the fillets on foil and cook for 7 to 8 minutes on each side, or until the fish is tender when pierced with a fork. 3. Top each piece of fish with ¼ cup Peach-Mango Salsa. Serve.

Per Serving: Calories 287; Fat 10.15g; Sodium 548mg; Carbs 15.34g; Fiber 2.3g; Sugar 11.27g; Protein 35.58g

Spicy Garlic Shrimp

Prep Time: 10 minutes | Cook Time: 3 minutes | Serves: 4

1 tablespoon olive oil

10 medium cloves garlic, peeled and chopped

1 pound extra-large shrimp (approximately 26–30), shelled and deveined

¼ teaspoon kosher salt

½ teaspoon ground paprika

¼ teaspoon red pepper flakes

1. In a medium sauté pan over medium heat, heat the oil. Add the garlic and sauté until fragrant but not brown, approximately 30 seconds. 2. Add the shrimp and salt and stir frequently until shrimp is cooked through, approximately 3 minutes. 3. Remove the pan from heat and stir in the paprika. Add the red pepper flakes and serve.

Per Serving: Calories 139; Fat 4.04g; Sodium 282mg; Carbs 2.91g; Fiber 0.3g; Sugar 0.25g; Protein 23.37g

Chapter 6 Meat Mains

Lamb Patties

1 pound ground lamb

½ small red onion, grated

1 tablespoon dried parsley

1 teaspoon dried oregano

1 teaspoon ground cumin

1 teaspoon garlic powder

½ teaspoon dried mint

¼ teaspoon paprika

¼ teaspoon kosher salt

⅛ teaspoon freshly ground black pepper

Extra-virgin olive oil, for panfrying

1. In a bowl, combine the lamb, parsley, onion, oregano, cumin, garlic powder, mint, paprika, salt, and pepper. Divide the meat into 4 small balls and work into smooth discs. 2. In a large sauté pan or skillet, heat a drizzle of olive oil over medium heat or brush a grill with the oil and set it to medium. Cook the patties for 4 to 5 minutes on each side, until cooked through and juices run clear. 3. Serve and enjoy.

Per Serving: Calories 232; Fat 14.51g; Sodium 214mg; Carbs 2.16g; Fiber 0.6g; Sugar 0.46g; Protein 23.55g

Flank Steak with Artichokes

4 tablespoons grapeseed oil, divided

2 pounds flank steak

1 (14-ounce) can artichoke hearts, drained and roughly chopped

1 onion, diced

8 garlic cloves, chopped

1 (32-ounce) container low-sodium beef broth

1 (14.5-ounce) can diced tomatoes, drained

1 cup tomato sauce

2 tablespoons tomato paste

1 teaspoon dried oregano

1 teaspoon dried parsley

1 teaspoon dried basil

½ teaspoon ground cumin

3 bay leaves

1. Preheat the oven to 450°F. 2. In an oven-safe sauté pan or skillet, heat 3 tablespoons of oil on medium heat. Sear the steak for 2 minutes per side on both sides. Transfer the steak to the oven for 30 minutes, or until desired tenderness. 3. Meanwhile, in a large pot, combine the remaining 1 tablespoon of oil, artichoke hearts, onion, and garlic. Pour in the beef broth, tomatoes, tomato sauce, and tomato paste. Stir in the oregano, parsley, basil, cumin, and bay leaves. 4. Cook the vegetables, covered, for 30 minutes. Remove the bay leaf and serve with the flank steak.

Per Serving: Calories 374; Fat 17.62g; Sodium 960mg; Carbs 17.07g; Fiber 8.5g; Sugar 5.34g; Protein 37.87g

Grilled Steak, Mushroom, and Onion Kebabs

Prep Time: 10 minutes | Cook Time: 10 minutes | Serves: 4

Nonstick cooking spray

4 garlic cloves, peeled

2 fresh rosemary sprigs (about 3 inches each)

2 tablespoons extra-virgin olive oil, divided

1 pound boneless top sirloin steak, about 1 inch thick

1 (8-ounce) package white button mushrooms

1 medium red onion, cut into 12 thin wedges

¼ teaspoon coarsely ground black pepper

2 tablespoons red wine vinegar

¼ teaspoon kosher or sea salt

1. Soak 12 (10-inch) wooden skewers in water. Coat the cold grill with nonstick cooking spray, and heat the grill to medium-high. 2. Cut a piece of aluminum foil into a 10-inch square. Place the garlic and rosemary sprigs in the center, drizzle with 1 tablespoon of oil, and wrap tightly to form a foil packet. Place the packet on the grill and close the grill cover. 3. Cut the steak into 1-inch cubes. Thread the beef onto the wet skewers, alternating with whole mushrooms and onion wedges. Spray the kebabs thoroughly with nonstick cooking spray, and sprinkle with the pepper. 4. Cook the kebabs on the covered grill for 4 to 5 minutes. Turn and grill for 4 to 5 more minutes, covered, until a meat thermometer inserted in the meat registers 145°F (medium rare) or 160°F (medium). 5. Remove the foil packet from the grill, open, and, using tongs, place the garlic and rosemary sprigs in a small bowl. Carefully strip the rosemary sprigs of their leaves into the bowl and pour in any accumulated juices and oil from the foil packet. Add the remaining 1 tablespoon of oil and the vinegar and salt. Mash the garlic with a fork and mix all ingredients in the bowl together. Pour over the finished steak kebabs and serve.

Per Serving: Calories 305; Fat 19.69g; Sodium 211mg; Carbs 5.61g; Fiber 1.2g; Sugar 2.32g; Protein 25.73g

Sirloin Steak with Sweet Bell Peppers

Prep Time: 20 minutes | Cook Time: 8 minutes | Serves: 4

12 ounces boneless top sirloin steak, about 1-inch thick, trimmed of visible fat

1 tablespoon olive oil, divided

Sea salt

Freshly ground black pepper

1 yellow bell pepper, thinly sliced

1 red bell pepper, thinly sliced

1 orange bell pepper, thinly sliced

1 small red onion, thinly sliced

4 garlic cloves, crushed

Juice of 1 lemon

1. Preheat the oven to broil. 2. Lightly oil the steak on both sides with 1 teaspoon of olive oil and season with the salt and pepper. Place the steak on a baking sheet. 3. In a large bowl, toss together the onion, garlic, bell peppers, and remaining 2 teaspoons of olive oil. Season lightly with the salt and pepper. Lay the vegetables flat on the baking sheet around the steak. 4. Broil the steak and vegetables until the steak is browned and the desired doneness, turning once, about 4 minutes per side. 5. Remove from the oven and let the steak rest for 10 minutes. Slice thinly on the bias against the grain. Drizzle the vegetables with the lemon juice and serve.

Per Serving: Calories 227; Fat 13.08g; Sodium 340mg; Carbs 8.64g; Fiber 1.2g; Sugar 2.25g; Protein 18.95g

Halibut with Olive-Tomato Sauce

Prep Time: 15 minutes | Cook Time: 25 minutes | Serves: 4

4 (4-ounce) halibut fillets

2 teaspoons ground cumin

Sea salt

1 tablespoon olive oil, divided

½ red onion, thinly sliced

2 teaspoons minced garlic

4 large tomatoes, chopped

½ cup chopped roasted red peppers

¼ cup pitted, chopped Kalamata olives

1 tablespoon chopped fresh oregano

Pinch red pepper flakes

1 tablespoon chopped fresh parsley

1. Season the halibut with the cumin and salt. 2. In a large skillet, heat 2 teaspoons of olive oil over medium-high heat. Cook the fish until it flakes easily, turning once, about 12 minutes total. Set aside. 3. Add the remaining 1 teaspoon of olive oil to the skillet and sauté the onion and garlic until softened, about 2 minutes. 4. Stir in the tomatoes, roasted red peppers, olives, oregano, and red pepper flakes and reduce the heat to medium low. Cook, stirring, until the sauce is well blended and heated through, about 10 minutes. Serve the fish topped with sauce and parsley.

Per Serving: Calories 302; Fat 20.6g; Sodium 511mg; Carbs 11.57g; Fiber 3.3g; Sugar 6.46g; Protein 18.69g

Lamb and Cauliflower Pilaff

Prep Time: 5 minutes | Cook Time: 17-27 minutes | Serves: 4

3 tablespoons extra virgin olive oil

1 onion or leek, finely chopped

1 fat garlic clove, crushed

200g (7oz) lamb mince

approx. 240g (8½oz) chicken livers or merguez sausages

400g (14oz) cauliflower, riced

1–2 tablespoons harissa paste

1 teaspoon ground cumin

100ml (3½fl oz) meat stock, hot water or leftover gravy

2 tablespoons finely chopped herbs, such as coriander, dill or

flat-leaf parsley

Salt and freshly ground black pepper

1. Pour the oil into a large frying pan over a medium heat, add the onion, and sweat for 5 minutes. Add a little seasoning, the garlic and mince and stir through to break up the mince. 2. Cut any tough, white, connective tissue away from the chicken livers and roughly chop them or, if using sausages, chop them into bite-sized pieces. Increase the heat and add the livers or sausages and cook for 7 to 10 minutes until brown all over and cooked through. 3. Stir in the cauliflower rice, harissa and cumin and stock, cover and cook for 5 minutes over a medium heat. Check a couple of times, you may need more stock or a splash of water if things look dry. You should see the cauliflower rice change from bright white grains to soft creamy-coloured ones. Taste and add seasoning if necessary. Fold in the herbs and serve straight from the pan into warm bowls.

Per Serving: Calories 290; Fat 18.12g; Sodium 407mg; Carbs 9.53g; Fiber 2.8g; Sugar 3.6g; Protein 22.81g

Chili-Spiced Lamb Chops

Prep Time: 2 minutes | Cook Time: 10 minutes | Serves: 4

4 (4-ounce) loin lamb chops with bones, trimmed

Sea salt

Freshly ground black pepper

1 tablespoon olive oil

2 tablespoons Sriracha sauce

1 tablespoon chopped fresh cilantro

1. Preheat the oven to 450°F. 2. Lightly season the lamb chops with the salt and pepper. 3. In a large ovenproof skillet, heat the olive oil over medium-high heat. Brown the chops on both sides, about 2 minutes per side, and spread the chops with sriracha. 4. Place the skillet in the oven and roast until the desired doneness, 4 to 5 minutes for medium. Serve topped with the cilantro.

Per Serving: Calories 176; Fat 8.66g; Sodium 428mg; Carbs 0.81g; Fiber 0.2g; Sugar 0.36g; Protein 24.1g

Pork Loin Gremolata

Prep Time: 15 minutes | Cook Time: 40 minutes | Serves: 4-6

1 cup water

One 3- to 4-pound boneless pork loin roast

2 tablespoons extra-virgin olive oil, plus more to oil the roasting pan

Gremolata:

2 garlic cloves, minced

1 bunch flatleaf parsley, stemmed and finely chopped

Zest and juice of 1 lemon

1½ teaspoons salt

½ teaspoon freshly ground black pepper

¼ teaspoon ground nutmeg

2 teaspoons extra-virgin olive oil

½ teaspoon salt

1. Preheat the oven to 400°F. 2. Oil a roasting pan big enough to hold the pork roast. Pour 1 cup water to the roasting pan. 3. Rub the roast with the olive oil and top with the salt, pepper, and nutmeg. 4. Roast 40 minutes, or until a meat thermometer reads 150°F. 5. Remove from the oven and allow to rest 10 to 15 minutes before serving. 6. To serve, cut the pork roast into ¼-inch slices and arrange on a platter. Spoon the gremolata over the top, or serve it on the side. 7. Roast pork will last in the refrigerator for about 1 week. Gremolata will last 1 week in the refrigerator or a few months in the freezer.

To make the gremolata:1. Combine the garlic, parsley, olive oil, lemon zest and juice, and salt in a small bowl and mix well. 2. Gremolata will last about 5 days in the refrigerator, or several months frozen.

Per Serving: Calories 411; Fat 16.89g; Sodium 1062mg; Carbs 1.85g; Fiber 0.6g; Sugar 0.34g; Protein 59.67g

Oregano Roasted Rib Eye Steak with Onions

1 pound rib eye steak, cubed

2 garlic cloves, minced

2 tablespoons olive oil

1 tablespoon fresh oregano

1 teaspoon salt

½ teaspoon black pepper

1 yellow onion, thinly sliced

1. Preheat the air fryer to 380°F. 2. In a medium bowl, combine the steak, garlic, olive oil, oregano, salt, pepper, and onion. Mix until all of the beef and onion are well coated. 3. Put the seasoned steak mixture into the air fryer basket. Roast for 5 minutes. Stir and roast for 5 minutes more. 4. Allow to rest for 5 minutes before serving with some favorite sides.

Per Serving: Calories 259; Fat 16.46g; Sodium 647mg; Carbs 3.65g; Fiber 0.8g; Sugar 1.2g; Protein 24.79g

Tuscan Steak with Salsa Verde

2 (18-ounce) bone-in rib eye steaks, about 1½ inches thick

2 tablespoons extra-virgin olive oil

For the Salsa Verde:

2 bunches flatleaf parsley, stems removed

½ cup pine nuts (pignoli)

5 small gherkins

8 pitted green olives

3 garlic cloves, crushed

1½ teaspoons salt

½ teaspoon freshly ground black pepper

3 tablespoons white wine vinegar

1 teaspoon salt

¼ teaspoon freshly ground black pepper

1 cup extra-virgin olive oil

1. Preheat the oven to 400°F. 2. Rub the steaks with the olive oil and sprinkle with the salt and pepper. 3. Place a large heavy skillet over high heat and let the pan get hot. To test, flick a few drops of water onto the pan. The water should immediately pop and evaporate; that's how you know the pan is ready. 4. Place the steaks in the pan and brown for 3 to 4 minutes or until they are a deep golden brown on each side. 5. Place the steaks on a rimmed baking sheet and slide it into the oven. Cook 10 minutes for rare or 15 minutes for medium. 6. Remove from the oven and let rest 10 to 15 minutes. Slice thin and serve with the Salsa Verde. 7. Once cooked, the steaks will keep for 5 days in the refrigerator.

To make the salsa verde: 1. Add all ingredients except the olive oil in a food processor or blender and pulse until finely chopped. 2. With the machine running, gradually pour in the olive oil in a thin stream. 3. After all the olive oil has been added, store the sauce in a jar in the refrigerator. 4. The salsa verde can be made ahead and stored in the refrigerator for several weeks, or can be frozen for several months.

Per Serving: Calories 676; Fat 66.65g; Sodium 1133mg; Carbs 5.04g; Fiber 0.8g; Sugar 2.73g; Protein 17.06g

Spice-Rubbed Pork Tenderloin

Prep Time: 5 minutes | Cook Time: 15 minutes | Serves: 4

1 teaspoon ground cinnamon

½ teaspoon ground cumin

½ teaspoon ground coriander

¼ teaspoon paprika

¼ teaspoon garlic powder

¼ teaspoon ground ginger

1 (1-pound) pork tenderloin

2 teaspoons olive oil

1. In a small bowl, combine the cumin, cinnamon, coriander, paprika, garlic powder, and ginger. 2. Rub the spice mixture generously all over the pork. 3. In a large skillet, heat the oil over medium-high heat. Cook the tenderloin for about 15 minutes, until it is browned on all sides and just cooked through. 4. Rest the meat on a cutting board for 10 minutes before slicing. Serve.

Per Serving: Calories 151; Fat 5.03g; Sodium 61mg; Carbs 1.65g; Fiber 0g; Sugar 0.04g; Protein 24.05g

Lebanese Beef Kebabs with Pickled Red Onions

Prep Time: 20 minutes | Cook Time: 10 minutes | Serves: 4

1 red bell pepper, chopped

½ onion, coarsely chopped

2 garlic cloves, coarsely chopped

1 pound ground beef

1½ teaspoons ground cumin

1½ teaspoons sumac (optional)

1½ teaspoons red pepper flakes

1 teaspoon kosher salt

Freshly ground black pepper

1 tablespoon ice-cold water

8 (12-inch) metal skewers (or wooden skewers soaked in warm water for 10 to 30 minutes)

1 teaspoon vegetable oil

1 recipe Pickled Red Onions

1. Place the red pepper, onion, and garlic in a food processor and pulse a few times until they're very finely chopped but not pureed. Set aside in a bowl, draining off any excess liquid. 2. Put the beef, processed vegetables, cumin, sumac (if using), red pepper flakes, salt, and a pinch of black pepper into the bowl of a stand mixer with the paddle attached. Mix on medium speed until the mixture begins sticking to the sides of the bowl, about a minute. Add the ice-cold water and mix for another 5 minutes, until you have a sticky mass. Chill the meat mixture in the freezer for a few minutes or in the refrigerator for at least 30 minutes (or overnight). 3. Divide the meat mixture into 8 balls. With a small bowl of cold water beside you, wet your hands and form the kebab mixture around the skewers, distributing it evenly until you have kofta about 9-by-2-inches thick. Smooth out any holes or tears, then place them on a greaseproof paper–lined baking sheet. (Refrigerate the kofta, covered, if you're not cooking them right away.) 4. Grease a grill pan with the vegetable oil and place it over high heat. Once the pan is hot, grill the kofta until charred on the outside and just cooked through (adjust the heat as necessary), 8 to 10 minutes. Put the grilled kebabs directly on top of the pickled red onions on a platter or individual plates, so the juices drip onto the onions, and serve immediately.

Per Serving: Calories 202; Fat 7.22g; Sodium 664mg; Carbs 7.29g; Fiber 1.4g; Sugar 2.69g; Protein 25.37g

Sautéed Pork Loin with Pears

Prep Time: 10 minutes | Cook Time: 18 minutes | Serves: 4

1 pound boneless pork loin, thinly sliced

Sea salt

Freshly ground black pepper

1 tablespoon olive oil

3 large pears, cored and cut into 1-inch chunks

½ sweet onion, chopped

1 teaspoon peeled and grated fresh ginger

¼ cup unsweetened apple juice

1 teaspoon chopped fresh thyme

1. Season the pork lightly with the salt and pepper. 2. In a large skillet, heat the oil over medium-high heat. Sauté the pork for about 6 minutes, until it is browned and just cooked through. Transfer the pork to a plate with a slotted spoon and set it aside. 3. Add the pears, onion, and ginger and sauté for about 7 minutes, until lightly caramelized. Add the pork back to the skillet along with the apple juice and thyme and simmer for 5 minutes. 4. Serve with your favorite cooked grains or a mixed green salad.

Per Serving: Calories 240; Fat 8.26g; Sodium 350mg; Carbs 14.95g; Fiber 3.8g; Sugar 10.03g; Protein 26.25g

Herbed Pork Cutlets and Roasted Asparagus

Prep Time: 10 minutes | Cook Time: 10 minutes | Serves: 4

2 tablespoons plus 1 teaspoon olive oil, divided

Juice of 2 limes, divided

1 tablespoon chopped fresh cilantro

1 tablespoon chopped fresh parsley

2 teaspoons minced garlic

4 (4-ounce) boneless center cut pork chops, pounded to ¼-inch thick

Sea salt

Freshly ground black pepper

3 asparagus bunches (about 36 stalks), woody ends trimmed

1. In a large bowl, combine 2 tablespoons oil, the juice from 1 lime, the cilantro, parsley, and garlic until well mixed. Add the pork and toss to coat. Season lightly with the salt and pepper. Let it rest 30 minutes at room temperature if you have set aside additional time to marinate. 2. Preheat the oven to broil and set the rack in the middle. 3. Heat a large skillet over medium-high heat and fry the pork chops for about 8 minutes in total, turning halfway through, until just cooked through and still juicy. 4. While the pork chops are cooking, arrange the asparagus on a baking sheet, drizzle with the remaining 1 teaspoon of olive oil, and season with the salt and pepper. Broil for about 2 minutes, until tender. Remove and drizzle with the remaining lime juice. 5. Serve each pork chop with a portion of asparagus.

Per Serving: Calories 277; Fat 9.22g; Sodium 394mg; Carbs 8.16g; Fiber 3.3g; Sugar 3.11g; Protein 40.82g

Sesame Pork Lettuce Wraps

1 tablespoon sesame oil

12 ounces ground pork

2 cups bean sprouts

1 red bell pepper, seeded and chopped

2 scallions, both white and green parts, chopped

⅛ teaspoon red pepper flakes

8 butter or iceberg lettuce leaves

Sesame seeds, for garnish

Lime wedges, for garnish

1. In a large skillet, heat the oil over medium-high heat. Sauté the pork for about 7 minutes, until it is cooked through. 2. Add the bean sprouts, bell pepper, and scallions and sauté for about 10 minutes, until softened. 3. Add the red pepper flakes and toss to mix. 4. Scoop the mixture evenly among the lettuce leaves and serve topped with sesame seeds, with lime wedges on the side.

Per Serving: Calories 281; Fat 21.76g; Sodium 56mg; Carbs 5.34g; Fiber 1.4g; Sugar 1.62g; Protein 16.94g

Spicy Beef Chili

2 teaspoons olive oil

12 ounces 93 percent lean ground beef

1 onion, chopped

1 green bell pepper, seeded and chopped

2 teaspoons minced garlic

1 (28-ounce) can no-salt-added diced tomatoes, drained

1 (15-ounce) can low-sodium black beans, drained and rinsed

1 (15-ounce) can low-sodium cannellini beans, drained

2 tablespoons chili powder

1. In a large saucepan, heat the oil over medium-high heat and sauté the ground beef for about 6 minutes, until it is cooked through. Add the bell pepper, onion, and garlic and sauté for about 4 minutes, until softened. 2. Add the tomatoes, black beans, cannellini beans, and chili powder and simmer for 10 minutes. 3. Serve.

Per Serving: Calories 376; Fat 8.53g; Sodium 495mg; Carbs 46.71g; Fiber 18.1g; Sugar 8.43g; Protein 32.23g

Roasted Steak and Broccoli

Prep Time: 15 minutes | Cook Time: 10 minutes | Serves: 4

2 (8-ounce) sirloin steaks, about 1-inch thick, trimmed of visible fat

1 tablespoon olive oil, divided

Sea salt

Freshly ground black pepper

2 broccoli heads, cut into florets

1 small red onion, thinly sliced

Juice of 1 lemon

1. Preheat the oven to 450°F. Line a baking sheet with foil. 2. Cover the steaks with 1 teaspoon of oil and season all over with the salt and pepper. 3. Place the steaks on one-third of the baking sheet. 4. In a large bowl, toss the onion, broccoli, and remaining 2 teaspoons of oil. Season lightly with the salt and pepper. 5. Spread the vegetables on the other two-thirds of the baking sheet. 6. Roast the steaks and vegetables, turning once, about 4 minutes per side for medium-rare, until the steaks are browned and have reached the desired doneness. 7. Let the steaks rest for 10 minutes and slice thinly on a bias against the grain. Drizzle the broccoli with the lemon juice. Serve.

Per Serving: Calories 254; Fat 8.2g; Sodium 422mg; Carbs 16.21g; Fiber 5.7g; Sugar 4.52g; Protein 31.28g

Mexican-Style Ground Beef

Prep Time: 15 minutes | Cook Time: 1 hour 20 minutes | Serves: 16

3 lb lean ground beef (at least 80%)

3/4 cup water

1 batch Salt-Free Taco Seasoning Mix

1. In 5-quart Dutch oven, cook the beef over medium-high heat about 10 minutes, stirring occasionally, or until thoroughly cooked; drain. 2. Reduce the heat to medium. Stir in the water and seasoning mix. Cook 3 to 5 minutes, stirring frequently, or until the liquid is absorbed and flavors are blended. Cool for 5 minutes. 3. Line 15×10×1-inch pan with foil. Spread the beef in the pan. Freeze about 1 hour, stirring once, until firm. 4. Place 2 cups of the beef mixture in each freezer-safe food storage container or resealable freezer plastic bag; seal tightly. Freeze up to 3 months.

Per Serving: Calories 160; Fat 8.9g; Sodium 87mg; Carbs 1.88g; Fiber 0.8g; Sugar 0.2g; Protein 17.49g

Homemade Italian Sausage

2 pounds (32 ounces) pork shoulder

1 teaspoon ground black pepper

1 teaspoon dried parsley

1 teaspoon Italian-style seasoning

1 teaspoon garlic powder

¾ teaspoon crushed anise seeds

⅛ teaspoon crushed red pepper flakes

½ teaspoon paprika

½ teaspoon instant minced onion flakes

1 teaspoon kosher or sea salt (optional)

1. Remove all fat from meat and cut the meat into cubes. Put in food processor and grind to desired consistency. 2. Add the remaining ingredients and mix until well blended. You can put sausage mixture in casings, but it works equally well broiled or grilled as patties. 3. Cook the sausage for about 10 minutes and serve.

Per Serving: Calories 311; Fat 13.13g; Sodium 786mg; Carbs 2.27g; Fiber 0.7g; Sugar 0.25g; Protein 43.05g

Rosemary-Citrus Roasted Pork Tenderloin

¼ cup olive oil

¼ cup chopped fresh rosemary

Juice of 1 lemon

Juice and zest of 1 lime

1 teaspoon minced garlic

1 teaspoon ground cumin

Sea salt

12 ounces boneless pork tenderloin

1. In a medium bowl, stir together the olive oil, rosemary, lemon juice, lime juice, lime zest, garlic, and cumin. Season with the salt. Add the pork tenderloin to the bowl, turning to coat. Cover and refrigerate for 1 hour. 2. Preheat a grill to medium-high heat. 3. Grill the tenderloin, turning several times and basting with the remaining marinade until it is cooked through (internal temperature: 140°F), 15 to 20 minutes. 4. Remove the tenderloin from the grill, cover it with foil, and let rest for 10 minutes. Serve.

Per Serving: Calories 225; Fat 15.63g; Sodium 338mg; Carbs 3.41g; Fiber 0.8g; Sugar 0.6g; Protein 18.17g

Miso Skirt Steak

3 tablespoons yellow miso

1 tablespoon tamari

½ tablespoon sesame oil

2 tablespoons chile-garlic sauce

1½ pounds skirt steak, patted dry

3 tablespoons rice vinegar

1 tablespoon vegetable oil, divided

1. In a medium bowl, stir together the miso, tamari, sesame oil, and chile-garlic sauce. Put 1 tablespoon of the sauce in a separate small bowl and set aside. Place the steak in the bowl with the remaining sauce and marinate it at room temperature for 10 to 15 minutes. 2. Stir the vinegar and ½ tablespoon of vegetable oil into the reserved sauce and set aside. 3. Remove the steak from the bowl and pat it dry 4. In a large skillet over medium-high heat, heat the remaining ½ tablespoons of vegetable oil, add the steak, and cook without disturbing it. Cook for 2 to 3 minutes, until brown. Flip the steak and repeat with the other side (bring to 125°F internal temperature for medium rare and 135°F for medium). Transfer the steak to a plate, tent with foil, and allow to rest for 5 to 10 minutes. 5. Serve with the sauce on the side.

Per Serving: Calories 373; Fat 22.99g; Sodium 865mg; Carbs 4.24g; Fiber 0.7g; Sugar 1.02g; Protein 37.71g

Chapter 7 Soups, Stews, and Salads

Curry Zucchini Soup

Prep Time: 10 minutes | Cook Time: 20 minutes | Serves: 4-6

¼ cup extra-virgin olive oil

1 medium onion, chopped (about ½ cup)

1 carrot, shredded

1 small garlic clove, minced

4 cups low-sodium chicken broth

2 medium zucchini, thinly sliced

2 apples, peeled and chopped

2½ teaspoons curry powder

¼ teaspoon salt

1. In a large pot, heat the oil over medium heat. Sauté the onion, carrot, and garlic and cook until tender. Add the chicken broth, zucchini, apples, and curry powder. 2. Boil for 2 minutes, reduce the heat, and simmer for 20 minutes, until the vegetables are tender. 3. Season with the salt and serve.

Per Serving: Calories 162; Fat 10.49g; Sodium 156mg; Carbs 14.44g; Fiber 2.6g; Sugar 6.92g; Protein 5.84g

White Bean and Kale Soup

Prep Time: 25 minutes | Cook Time: 30 minutes | Serves: 4

1 to 2 tablespoons extra-virgin olive oil

1 large shallot, minced

1 large purple carrot, chopped

1 celery stalk, chopped

1 teaspoon garlic powder

3 cups low-sodium vegetable broth

1 (15-ounce) can cannellini beans

1 cup chopped baby kale

1 teaspoon salt (optional)

½ teaspoon freshly ground black pepper (optional)

1 lemon, juiced and zested

1½ tablespoons chopped fresh thyme (optional)

3 tablespoons chopped fresh oregano (optional)

1. In a large, deep pot, heat the olive oil. Add the shallot, carrot, celery, and garlic powder and sauté on medium-low heat for 3 to 5 minutes, until the vegetables are golden. 2. Add the vegetable broth and beans and bring to a simmer. Cook for 15 minutes. 3. Add in the kale, salt (if using), and pepper (if using). Cook for another 5 to 10 minutes, until the kale is soft. Right before serving, stir in the lemon juice and zest, thyme (if using), and oregano (if using).

Per Serving: Calories 154; Fat 7.24g; Sodium 1027mg; Carbs 20.21g; Fiber 5.4g; Sugar 5.03g; Protein 5.09g

Yellow and White Hearts of Palm Salad

Prep Time: 10 minutes | Cook Time: 0 minute | Serves: 4

2 (14-ounce) cans hearts of palm, drained and cut into ½-inch-thick slices

1 avocado, cut into ½-inch pieces

1 cup halved yellow cherry tomatoes

½ small shallot, thinly sliced

⅛ teaspoon freshly ground black pepper

¼ cup coarsely chopped flat-leaf parsley

2 tablespoons low-fat mayonnaise

2 tablespoons extra-virgin olive oil

¼ teaspoon salt

1. In a large bowl, toss the hearts of palm, avocado, tomatoes, shallot, and parsley. 2. In a small bowl, whisk the mayonnaise, olive oil, salt, and pepper, then mix into the large bowl. 3. Serve and enjoy.

Per Serving: Calories 281; Fat 15.83g; Sodium 185mg; Carbs 32.89g; Fiber 5.4g; Sugar 17.78g; Protein 4.37g

Golden Gazpacho

Prep Time: 20 minutes | Cook Time: 0 minute | Serves: 4

1½ pounds golden tomatoes, cored and cut into 8 wedges

1 cucumber, peeled, seeded, and coarsely chopped

1 yellow bell pepper, seeded and chopped

½ cup chopped red onion

1 small red chile pepper, seeded and chopped (optional)

1 garlic clove, sliced

¼ cup extra-virgin olive oil

2 tablespoons lemon juice

1 teaspoon salt

½ teaspoon ground cumin

½ teaspoon ground turmeric

¼ teaspoon freshly ground black pepper

2 tablespoons finely chopped fresh cilantro

1. Place the tomatoes, cucumber, bell pepper, red onion, chile pepper (if using), garlic, olive oil, and lemon juice in a large bowl and mix to combine. 2. In a food processor or blender, purée the vegetables in batches. Gazpacho can be as smooth or as chunky as you'd like. 3. When it's all been puréed, add the salt, cumin, turmeric, and pepper. 4. Ladle into bowls and garnish with the chopped cilantro. 5. Gazpacho can be stored in the fridge for about 3 days (any longer and the flavors diminish) or frozen for several months. If freezing, don't add the cilantro since it will lose its fresh flavor; add it when ready to serve.

Per Serving: Calories 180; Fat 14.29g; Sodium 625mg; Carbs 12.81g; Fiber 2.8g; Sugar 2.3g; Protein 2.96g

Italian Orange and Celery Salad

Prep Time: 15 minutes | Cook Time: 0 minute | Serves: 2

3 celery stalks, including leaves, sliced diagonally into ½-inch slices

2 large oranges, peeled and sliced into rounds

½ cup green olives (or any variety)

¼ cup sliced red onion (about ¼ onion)

1 tablespoon extra-virgin olive oil

1 tablespoon olive brine

1 tablespoon freshly squeezed lemon or orange juice (from ½ small lemon or 1 orange round)

¼ teaspoon kosher or sea salt

¼ teaspoon freshly ground black pepper

1. Place the celery, oranges, olives, and onion on a large serving platter or in a shallow, wide bowl. 2. In a small bowl, whisk together the oil, olive brine, and lemon juice. Pour over the salad, sprinkle with salt and pepper, and serve.

Per Serving: Calories 153; Fat 10.67g; Sodium 592mg; Carbs 14.35g; Fiber 2.1g; Sugar 8.83g; Protein 1.35g

Mediterranean Potato Salad

Prep Time: 10 minutes | Cook Time: 20 minutes | Serves: 6

2 pounds Yukon Gold baby potatoes, cut into 1-inch cubes

3 tablespoons freshly squeezed lemon juice (from about 1 medium lemon)

3 tablespoons extra-virgin olive oil

1 tablespoon olive brine

¼ teaspoon kosher or sea salt

1 (2.25-ounce) can sliced olives (about ½ cup)

1 cup sliced celery (about 2 stalks) or fennel

2 tablespoons chopped fresh oregano

2 tablespoons torn fresh mint

1. In a medium saucepan, cover the potatoes with cold water until the waterline is one inch above the potatoes. Set over high heat, bring the potatoes to a boil, then turn down the heat to medium-low. Simmer for 12 to 15 minutes, until the potatoes are just fork tender. 2. While the potatoes are cooking, in a small bowl, stir together the lemon juice, oil, olive brine, and salt. 3. Drain the potatoes in a colander and transfer to a serving bowl. Immediately pour about 3 tablespoons of the dressing over the potatoes. Gently mix in the olives and celery. 4. Before serving, gently mix in the oregano, mint, and the remaining dressing.

Per Serving: Calories 195; Fat 8.16g; Sodium 203mg; Carbs 28.41g; Fiber 4.2g; Sugar 1.57g; Protein 3.36g

Tomato and Lentil Soup

Prep Time: 10 minutes | Cook Time: 35 minutes | Serves: 4

1 tablespoon olive oil

1 sweet onion, chopped

2 celery stalks, chopped

1 tablespoon minced garlic

6 cups low-sodium vegetable stock

2 (28-ounce) cans low-sodium diced tomatoes

1 (15-ounce) can low-sodium red lentils, rinsed and drained

1 tablespoon chopped fresh basil

Pinch red pepper flakes

Sea salt

Freshly ground black pepper

1. In a large pot, heat the olive oil over medium-high heat. Sauté the onion, celery, and garlic until softened, about 3 minutes. 2. Stir in the stock and tomatoes with their juices and bring to a boil. Reduce the heat to low and simmer for 20 minutes. 3. In a food processor, purée the soup until smooth. Return the soup to the pot and stir in the lentils, basil, and red pepper flakes and simmer until heated through, about 10 minutes. Season with the pepper and salt and serve.

Per Serving: Calories 400; Fat 7.54g; Sodium 1444mg; Carbs 72.14g; Fiber 10.1g; Sugar 25.18g; Protein 19.43g

Fennel and Leek Broth

Prep Time: 10 minutes | Cook Time: 15 minutes | Serves: 4

2 large leeks, root and top trimmed, thinly sliced

1 large fennel bulb, stemmed and thinly sliced

1 garlic clove, thinly sliced

1 carrot, peeled and thinly sliced

1 thin slice fresh turmeric root

6 cups low-sodium vegetable or chicken broth

1 teaspoon salt

¼ teaspoon freshly ground black pepper

¼ cup chopped fresh flatleaf parsley

2 tablespoons chopped fresh dill

¼ cup extra-virgin olive oil

1. Place the leeks, fennel, garlic, carrot, and turmeric in a large pot. Add the broth, salt, and pepper. 2. Bring to a boil and reduce to a simmer. Cook for 5 to 10 minutes, or until the carrots are tender. 3. Ladle the soup into serving bowls and top with the parsley and dill. Drizzle with the olive oil and serve. 4. This soup will last in the refrigerator for 1 week and can be frozen for several months.

Per Serving: Calories 238; Fat 16.45g; Sodium 733mg; Carbs 17.86g; Fiber 3.7g; Sugar 4.6g; Protein 9.37g

Salmon, Citrus, and Avocado Salad

Prep Time: 20 minutes | Cook Time: 0 minute | Serves: 4

6 cups mixed baby greens (spinach, kale, and Swiss chard)

2 large oranges, peeled, segmented, and cut into chunks

2 ruby red grapefruits, peeled, segmented, and cut into chunks

1 avocado, peeled, pitted, and chopped

2 (5-ounce) cans boneless, skinless salmon, drained

½ cup pecan halves

½ cup Pesto Vinaigrette

1. Place the greens on a large platter and top with the oranges, grapefruits, avocado, salmon, and pecans. 2. Drizzle the salad with the vinaigrette and serve.

Per Serving: Calories 588; Fat 47.7g; Sodium 399mg; Carbs 25.45g; Fiber 7.8g; Sugar 15.63g; Protein 19.69g

White Beans and Chicken Stew

Prep Time: 15 minutes | Cook Time: 40 minutes | Serves: 4-6

¼ cup extra-virgin olive oil

4 boneless, skinless chicken breasts, cut into 1-inch pieces

1 onion, chopped

1 fennel bulb, chopped

2 garlic cloves, minced

2 celery stalks, chopped

2 large carrots, peeled and sliced into ¼-inch slices

1 teaspoon salt

¼ teaspoon freshly ground black pepper

1 sprig fresh rosemary

½ teaspoon ground turmeric

4 cups chicken broth

1 (15.5-ounce) can white beans, drained and rinsed

2 tablespoons chopped fresh basil

1. In a large Dutch oven or a heavy pot with a lid, heat the olive oil. 2. Add the chicken and brown on each side, about 1 minute per side. Remove the chicken and set aside. 3. Add the onion, fennel, garlic, and celery and sauté until lightly browned, about 7 minutes. 4. Add the carrots, salt, pepper, rosemary, and turmeric and sauté for an additional 2 minutes. 5. Return the chicken to the pan and add the broth. Bring to a boil, reduce to a simmer, and cook about 5 minutes, or until the chicken is cooked through. 6. Add the beans and cook for another minute or so to warm through. Remove the sprig of rosemary, add the chopped basil, and serve. 7. This dish can be made ahead and refrigerated for 5 days or frozen for several months. Add the fresh basil just before serving.

Per Serving: Calories 360; Fat 13.76g; Sodium 1406mg; Carbs 21.72g; Fiber 5.3g; Sugar 3.38g; Protein 39.05g

Moroccan Carrot Salad with Cinnamon

Prep Time: 10 minutes | Cook Time: 10 minutes | Serves: 4

3 tablespoons extra-virgin olive oil

2 large carrots, peeled and thinly sliced

1 garlic clove, crushed

1 teaspoon salt

¼ teaspoon freshly ground black pepper

½ teaspoon ground cinnamon

3 tablespoons orange juice

1. Place a large skillet over high heat, add the olive oil. When the skillet is hot, add the carrots. 2. Add the crushed garlic and sauté for about 10 minutes, or until the carrots are tender. 3. Add the salt, pepper, cinnamon, and orange juice, and cook 1 minute longer. 4. Spoon into a serving dish and serve. 5. This salad can be made several days ahead and kept covered in the fridge.

Per Serving: Calories 98; Fat 10.16g; Sodium 583mg; Carbs 1.96g; Fiber 0.6g; Sugar 1.06g; Protein 0.17g

Flavorful Fish Stew

Prep Time: 15 minutes | Cook Time: 30 minutes | Serves: 4-5

2 tablespoons olive oil

2 ounces pancetta, cubed

2 tomatoes on the vine, diced

1 onion, chopped

1 leek, white part only, sliced and rinsed well

3 garlic cloves, minced

1 tablespoon tomato paste

Sea salt

Freshly ground black pepper

¼ teaspoon saffron threads

4 cups fish stock

2 cups water

1 russet potato, peeled and cubed

½ teaspoon red pepper flakes

1 bay leaf

2 pounds prepackaged mixed seafood or your favorite fish, cut into 1-inch chunks

1. In a Dutch oven, heat the olive oil over medium-high heat. Add the pancetta, tomatoes, onion, leek, garlic, and tomato paste and sauté for 5 minutes. Season with the salt and black pepper. Add the saffron and sauté for 30 seconds. 2. Add the fish stock, water, potato, red pepper flakes, and bay leaf and bring the mixture to a boil. Reduce the heat to low and simmer until potato is tender, 15 to 20 minutes. 3. Increase the heat to medium and add the fish. Simmer for 5 to 10 minutes, until the fish is cooked through. Remove the bay leaf and serve. 4. Store leftover stew in an airtight container in the refrigerator for up to 4 days.

Per Serving: Calories 386; Fat 12.77g; Sodium 1283mg; Carbs 22.08g; Fiber 2.4g; Sugar 2.99g; Protein 44.48g

Herby Tomato Soup

Prep Time: 10 minutes | Cook Time: 10 minutes | Serves: 2

¼ cup extra-virgin olive oil

2 garlic cloves, minced

1 (14.5-ounce) can plum tomatoes, whole or diced

1 cup vegetable broth

¼ cup chopped fresh basil

1. In a medium pot, heat the oil over medium heat. Add the garlic and cook for 2 minutes, until fragrant. 2. Meanwhile, in a bowl using an immersion blender or in a blender, puree the tomatoes and their juices. 3. Add the pureed tomatoes and broth to the pot and mix well. Simmer for 10 to 15 minutes and serve, garnished with the basil.

Per Serving: Calories 143; Fat 12.15g; Sodium 469mg; Carbs 8.2g; Fiber 4g; Sugar 5.28g; Protein 2.02g

Chicken and Chickpea Stew

Prep Time: 15 minutes | Cook Time: 30 minutes | Serves: 4

3 tablespoons olive oil

1½ pounds chicken drumsticks

1 onion, chopped

2 leeks, white parts only, chopped and rinsed well

2 red bell peppers, chopped

1 carrot, chopped

4 garlic cloves, minced

Juice of ½ lemon

2 cups chicken broth

1 (15-ounce) can diced tomatoes

1 (15-ounce) can chickpeas, drained and rinsed

½ teaspoon red pepper flakes, or more if desired

½ teaspoon dried oregano

¼ teaspoon dried sage

¼ teaspoon dried rosemary

Sea salt

Freshly ground black pepper

1. In a large stockpot over medium heat, heat the olive oil. Add the chicken and cook, turning it frequently, for 10 minutes, or until browned. 2. Add the onion, leeks, bell peppers, carrot, garlic, and lemon juice and sauté for 5 minutes. Add the broth, tomatoes, chickpeas, red pepper flakes, oregano, sage, and rosemary. Bring to a boil and then reduce the heat to low. Cover and simmer for 15 to 20 minutes, until chicken is cooked through. 3. Season with the salt and black pepper and serve.4. Store leftover stew in an airtight container in the refrigerator for up to 4 days.

Per Serving: Calories 521; Fat 19.95g; Sodium 1318mg; Carbs 43.12g; Fiber 11.1g; Sugar 12.79g; Protein 44.04g

Mediterranean-Style Egg Salad

Prep Time: 25 minutes | Cook Time: 0 minute | Serves: 4

4 large hard-boiled eggs, peeled and chopped

2 medium Roma tomatoes, chopped

1 medium avocado, peeled, pitted, and chopped

⅓ cup sliced black olives

2 tablespoons finely minced red onion

2 tablespoons extra-virgin olive oil

1 tablespoon freshly squeezed lemon juice

¼ teaspoon salt

¼ teaspoon freshly ground black pepper

¼ cup chopped fresh parsley, for garnish (optional)

1. In a large bowl, combine the eggs, tomatoes, avocado, olives, onion, olive oil, lemon juice, salt, and pepper. Mix well. Garnish with the parsley (if using). 2. Serve right away or chill first. 3. Refrigerate any leftovers in an airtight container for up to 5 days.re

Per Serving: Calories 245; Fat 20.66g; Sodium 298mg; Carbs 8.98g; Fiber 4.7g; Sugar 2.85g; Protein 8.13g

Tuna, Tomato, and Egg Salad

Prep Time: 20 minutes | Cook Time: 0 minute | Serves: 4-6

1 (5-ounce) package baby spinach

2 (5-ounce) cans tuna packed in water, drained

4 medium ripe tomatoes, cored and cut into 1-inch cubes

1 red bell pepper, seeded and thinly sliced

½ red onion, thinly sliced

1 garlic clove, minced

½ cup pitted Niçoise olives

2 hard-boiled eggs, peeled and cut into quarters

2 tablespoons capers

¼ cup extra-virgin olive oil

2 tablespoons red wine vinegar

1 teaspoon salt

¼ teaspoon freshly ground black pepper

1. Place the baby spinach, tuna, tomatoes, bell pepper, onion, garlic, olives, eggs, capers, olive oil, salt, vinegar, and pepper in a large bowl and toss to combine. 2. Let sit for 5 to 10 minutes before serving to allow the flavors to develop. 3. Place in a serving bowl and serve immediately.

Per Serving: Calories 187; Fat 12.62g; Sodium 699mg; Carbs 6.82g; Fiber 2.2g; Sugar 3.25g; Protein 13.13g

Greens and Herbs Salad

2 large heads butter or Boston or Bibb lettuce, leaves removed, washed, and dried

2 radishes, thinly sliced

1 tablespoon chopped fresh chives

1 tablespoon chopped fresh flatleaf parsley

2 teaspoons chopped fresh tarragon

¼ cup extra-virgin olive oil

2 tablespoons lemon juice

1 teaspoon lemon zest

1 teaspoon salt

¼ teaspoon freshly ground black pepper

¼ cup chopped toasted walnuts or hazelnuts (optional)

1. Arrange the lettuce leaves in a serving platter or bowl. 2. Top with the radishes, chives, parsley, and tarragon. 3. Drizzle the olive oil and lemon juice over the lettuce. Sprinkle on the lemon zest, pepper, and salt and toss gently to coat the lettuce leaves. 4. Sprinkle the toasted nuts over the top (if using), and serve immediately.

Per Serving: Calories 112; Fat 6.22g; Sodium 620mg; Carbs 13.18g; Fiber 5.2g; Sugar 7.87g; Protein 4.69g

Fennel, Grapefruit, and Crab Salad with Parsley Lemon Dressing

1 head romaine lettuce, washed and chopped

1 fennel bulb, shaved or sliced very thin

1 large pink grapefruit, peeled and cut into ½-inch cubes

1 pound crabmeat

2 teaspoons salt, divided

¼ teaspoon freshly ground black pepper

⅓ cup extra-virgin olive oil

1 shallot, minced

1 teaspoon Dijon mustard

Zest and juice of 1 lemon

2 tablespoons chopped fresh flatleaf parsley

¼ teaspoon red pepper flakes

1. Place the lettuce on a large platter, top with the fennel, grapefruit, and crab, and sprinkle with 1 teaspoon of the salt and the pepper. 2. In a small bowl, stir together the olive oil, shallot, mustard, lemon zest and juice, parsley, 1 teaspoon salt, and the red pepper flakes until well combined. 3. Drizzle the dressing over the salad. 4. Any leftover dressing can be stored in the refrigerator for several days.

Per Serving: Calories 336; Fat 19.82g; Sodium 1554mg; Carbs 18.22g; Fiber 6.5g; Sugar 10.69g; Protein 23.96g

Fish Stew with Roasted Red Pepper Sauce

Prep Time: 15 minutes | Cook Time: 15 minutes | Serves: 4

2 tablespoons extra-virgin olive oil, plus more to drizzle

2 teaspoons paprika

½ teaspoon ground cumin

Several saffron threads (optional)

1 onion, chopped

1 garlic clove, minced

4 Roma tomatoes, cored and diced.

2 large red bell peppers, roasted, peeled, seeded, and chopped

½ cup water or chicken broth

1 teaspoon salt

1½ pounds firm-flesh fish, cut into 1-inch cubes

2 tablespoons fresh flatleaf parsley, chopped

1. Place a Dutch oven or a heavy pot with a lid over high heat. Add the olive oil, paprika, cumin, saffron (if using), onion, and garlic. Sauté for 5 minutes to soften the vegetables. Add the tomatoes, roasted peppers, water or broth, and salt, and simmer 10 minutes. 2. Pour the vegetables into a blender or food processor and process until smooth. Return the sauce to the pot and bring to a simmer. 3. Gently add the fish to the sauce, cover, and cook 5 minutes. 4. Ladle into bowls, drizzle with the olive oil, garnish with the parsley, and serve. 5. The sauce (without the fish) can be made ahead and stored in the refrigerator for 1 week, or frozen for several months. Once the stew has been made, it's best to eat it within 3 days or freeze it for 1 month.

Per Serving: Calories 226; Fat 8.03g; Sodium 1194mg; Carbs 10.81g; Fiber 2.9g; Sugar 6.15g; Protein 28.03g

Slow Cooker Vegetable Stock

Prep Time: 10 minutes | Cook Time: 6 hours | Serves: 6

2 leeks, root and top trimmed, cut in half lengthwise

1 fennel bulb, cut in half

1 onion, cut in half

2 carrots, peeled and cut into 2-inch pieces

1 head garlic, cut in half across the middle

4 sprigs fresh flatleaf parsley

1 sprig fresh rosemary

6 cups water

1. Place the leeks, fennel, onion, carrots, garlic, parsley, rosemary, and water in a slow cooker, cover, and cook on low for 6 hours. 2. Use a slotted spoon to remove all the vegetables. 3. Pour the remaining stock through a strainer set over a large bowl. 4. Pour the strained stock into jars or plastic containers to store. 5. Stock will last 1 week in the refrigerator or for several months in the freezer. Freeze it in 1- or 2-cup containers for easy thawing.

Per Serving: Calories 282; Fat 10.06g; Sodium 94mg; Carbs 49.35g; Fiber 26.4g; Sugar 6.48g; Protein 7.41g

Tuscan Vegetable Stew

Prep Time: 15 minutes | Cook Time: 15 minutes | Serves: 4-6

3 tablespoons extra-virgin olive oil

1 onion, chopped

2 garlic cloves, chopped

2 zucchini, chopped

1 bell pepper (any color), seeded and chopped

2 large tomatoes, chopped

1 carrot, peeled and chopped

4 cups vegetable broth

1 teaspoon salt

½ teaspoon freshly ground black pepper

½ teaspoon dried rosemary

1 (15.5-ounce) can white beans, drained and rinsed

1 (15.5-ounce) can black beans, drained and rinsed

½ cup chopped fresh flatleaf parsley

1. Place a Dutch oven or a heavy pot with a lid over high heat. Add the olive oil, onion, and garlic and sauté for 3 to 5 minutes, or until the onions have softened. 2. Add the zucchini, bell pepper, tomatoes, and carrot and sauté for an additional 3 minutes. 3. Add the broth, salt, pepper, and rosemary and bring to a boil. Reduce to a simmer and cook for 5 minutes. 4. Add the beans and cook for another minute or two to heat the beans through. 5. Ladle into bowls and garnish with the chopped parsley. 6. Store leftovers in the refrigerator for 5 days and frozen for several months.

Per Serving: Calories 313; Fat 9.07g; Sodium 1064mg; Carbs 45.98g; Fiber 12.9g; Sugar 5.78g; Protein 15.8g

Lamb and Bean Stew

Prep Time: 15 minutes | Cook Time: 35 minutes | Serves: 4

4 tablespoons olive oil, divided

1 pound lamb shoulder, cut into 2-inch cubes

Sea salt

Freshly ground black pepper

2 garlic cloves, minced (optional)

1 large onion, diced

1 cup chopped celery

1 cup chopped tomatoes

1 cup chopped carrots

⅓ cup tomato paste

1 (28-ounce) can white kidney beans, drained and rinsed

2 cups water

1. In a stockpot, heat 1 tablespoon of olive oil over medium-high heat. Season the lamb pieces with the pepper and salt and add to the stockpot with the garlic, if desired. Brown the lamb, turning it frequently, for 3 to 4 minutes. Add the remaining 3 tablespoons of olive oil, the onion, celery, tomatoes, and carrots and cook for 4 to 5 minutes. 2. Add the tomato paste and stir to combine, then add the beans and water. Bring the mixture to a boil and then reduce the heat to low. Cover and simmer for 25 minutes, or until the lamb is fully cooked. 3. Taste, adjust the seasoning, and serve. 4. Store leftovers in an airtight container in the refrigerator for up to 3 days.

Per Serving: Calories 519; Fat 24.44g; Sodium 1019mg; Carbs 41.92g; Fiber 11.8g; Sugar 10.55g; Protein 34.96g

Pork Stew with Leeks

Prep Time: 15 minutes | Cook Time: 55 minutes | Serves: 4

2 tablespoons olive oil

2 leeks, white parts only, chopped and rinsed well

1 onion, chopped

2 garlic cloves, minced

1 carrot, chopped

1 celery stalk, chopped

2 pounds boneless pork loin chops, cut into 2-inch pieces

4 cups beef broth

2 cups water

3 potatoes, peeled and chopped

1 tablespoon tomato paste

Sea salt

Freshly ground black pepper

1. In a large skillet, heat the olive oil over medium-high heat. Add the leeks, onion, and garlic and sauté for 5 minutes, or until softened. Add the carrot and celery and cook for 3 minutes. Add the pork, broth, water, potatoes, and tomato paste and bring to a boil. 2. Reduce the heat to low, cover, and simmer for 45 minutes, or until the pork is cooked through. Season to taste with the pepper and salt and serve. 3. Store leftovers in an airtight container in the refrigerator for up to 3 days.

Per Serving: Calories 523; Fat 15.35g; Sodium 1360mg; Carbs 37.75g; Fiber 5.1g; Sugar 5.63g; Protein 56.75g

Moroccan-Inspired Chicken Stew

Prep Time: 5 minutes | Cook Time: 15 minutes | Serves: 4-6

2 teaspoons ground cumin

1 teaspoon ground cinnamon

½ teaspoon turmeric

½ teaspoon paprika

1½ pounds boneless, skinless chicken, cut into strips

2 tablespoons extra-virgin olive oil

5 garlic cloves, smashed and coarsely chopped

2 onions, thinly sliced

1 tablespoon fresh lemon zest

½ cup coarsely chopped olives

2 cups low-sodium chicken broth

Cilantro, for garnish (optional)

1. In a medium bowl, whisk together the cumin, cinnamon, turmeric, and paprika until well blended. Add the chicken, tossing to coat, and set aside. 2. Heat the extra-virgin olive oil in a large skillet or medium Dutch oven over medium-high heat. Add the chicken and garlic in one layer and cook, browning on all sides, about 2 minutes. 3. Add the onions, lemon zest, olives, and broth and bring the soup to a boil. Reduce the heat to medium low, cover, and simmer for 8 minutes. 4. Uncover the soup and let it simmer for another 2 to 3 minutes for the sauce to thicken slightly. Adjust the seasonings as desired and serve garnished with the cilantro (if using). 5. Store the cooled soup in an airtight container in the refrigerator for up to 5 days.

Per Serving: Calories 212; Fat 9.36g; Sodium 159mg; Carbs 3.86g; Fiber 1g; Sugar 0.35g; Protein 27.61g

Chapter 8 Sauces, Dips, and Dressings

Classic Hummus

Prep Time: 15 minutes | Cook Time: 0 minute | Serves: 8

1 (15 ounce) can no-salt-added chickpeas, drained (liquid reserved) and rinsed

¼ cup ground flaxseed

2 tablespoons olive oil, plus more for drizzling on top

2 tablespoons freshly squeezed lemon juice

3 garlic cloves, peeled

½ teaspoon ground cumin

½ teaspoon salt

½ teaspoon sesame oil

1. Place the chickpeas and ¼ cup of the reserved liquid, olive oil, lemon juice, flaxseed, salt, garlic, cumin, and sesame oil in a food processor. Process until smooth and creamy. Pour in the additional reserved bean liquid until it reaches your desired consistency. 2. Transfer the hummus to a bowl. Drizzle with the additional olive oil and serve. 3. Store in an airtight container in the refrigerator for up to 7 days.

Per Serving: Calories 155; Fat 7.3g; Sodium 151mg; Carbs 16.79g; Fiber 5.5g; Sugar 2.74g; Protein 5.78g

Eggplant Relish Spread

Prep Time: 10 minutes | Cook Time: 20 minutes | Serves: 6

2 tablespoons extra-virgin olive oil

1 cup finely chopped onion (about ½ medium onion)

1 garlic clove, minced (about ½ teaspoon)

1 large globe eggplant, cut into ½-inch cubes (about 5 cups)

¼ teaspoon kosher or sea salt

1 (12-ounce) jar roasted red peppers, chopped

1½ cups chopped fresh tomatoes

½ cup balsamic or red wine vinegar

½ cup capers or chopped olives

1. In a large skillet over medium heat, heat the oil. 2. Add the onion and cook for 4 minutes, stirring occasionally. Add the garlic and cook for 1 minute, stirring often. Turn up the heat to medium-high, and add the eggplant and salt. Cook for 5 minutes, stirring occasionally. 3. Add the peppers, tomatoes, and vinegar, stir, and cover. Cook for 10 minutes, stirring every minute or so to prevent everything from sticking. If it looks like it's starting to stick and burn, turn down the heat to medium and add 1 tablespoon of water. 4. Remove from the heat, stir in the capers, and let sit for a few minutes to let the liquid absorb. Stir and serve, or store in a covered jar in the refrigerator for up to 10 days. It tastes even better the day after you make it!

Per Serving: Calories 106; Fat 6.14g; Sodium 962mg; Carbs 12.04g; Fiber 4.7g; Sugar 5.23g; Protein 2.09g

Pesto Vinaigrette

Prep Time: 10 minutes | Cook Time: 0 minute | Serves: 4

¼ cup apple cider vinegar

2 tablespoons basil pesto

½ cup olive oil

Sea salt

Freshly ground black pepper

1. In a medium bowl, stir the vinegar and pesto together until blended. Add the olive oil in a thin stream while whisking until the vinaigrette is emulsified and season with the salt and pepper. Store the dressing in a sealed container in the refrigerator for up to 1 week.

Per Serving: Calories 289; Fat 31.43g; Sodium 364mg; Carbs 2.26g; Fiber 0.2g; Sugar 1.56g; Protein 0.83g

Aioli

Prep Time: 15 minutes | Cook Time: 0 minute | Serves: 4

2 garlic cloves, peeled and crushed

1 teaspoon salt, divided

1 egg yolk

1 tablespoon lemon juice

½ teaspoon Dijon mustard

¼ teaspoon freshly ground black pepper

1 cup extra-virgin olive oil

3 tablespoons water

1. Arrange the garlic cloves on a cutting board, sprinkle with ½ teaspoon salt, and mash with the back of a spoon until the garlic is puréed. 2. In the bowl of a food processor, combine the lemon juice, garlic purée, mustard, egg yolk, the remaining ½ teaspoon salt, and pepper. 3. With the machine running, slowly drizzle the olive oil into the egg mixture. The mixture will become thick and creamy. When all the olive oil has been added, add the water a little bit at a time. 4. Spoon it into a jar with a tightly fitting lid and store it in the refrigerator. Aioli can keep 5 days in the refrigerator.

Per Serving: Calories 495; Fat 55.17g; Sodium 592mg; Carbs 1.04g; Fiber 0.1g; Sugar 0.14g; Protein 0.82g

Homemade Olive Oil Mayonnaise

1 egg yolk

1 tablespoon lemon juice

1 teaspoon Dijon mustard

1 teaspoon salt

¼ teaspoon freshly ground black pepper

1 cup extra-virgin olive oil

1. In the bowl of a food processor, combine the egg yolk, mustard, salt, lemon juice, and pepper. 2. With the machine running, slowly drizzle the olive oil into the egg mixture. The mixture will become thick and creamy. If the mayonnaise is too thick, thin it with a bit of water. 3. Spoon it into a jar with a tightly fitting lid and store it in the refrigerator. 4. Mayonnaise can last for 7 days in the refrigerator.

Per Serving: Calories 493; Fat 55.18g; Sodium 598mg; Carbs 0.59g; Fiber 0.1g; Sugar 0.13g; Protein 0.75g

Salt-Free Taco Seasoning Mix

2 tablespoons chili powder

1 tablespoon onion powder

5 teaspoons ground cumin

5 teaspoons paprika

2½ teaspoons garlic powder

⅛ to ¼ teaspoon ground red pepper (cayenne)

1. In a small container with tight-fitting lid, mix all ingredients until well blended. Cover and store in a cool, dry place up to 6 months. Stir or shake well before using.

Per Serving: Calories 42; Fat 1.57g; Sodium 123mg; Carbs 7.51g; Fiber 3.1g; Sugar 0.81g; Protein 1.92g

Peach-Mango Salsa

Prep Time: 10 minutes | Cook Time: 0 minute | Serves: 6

1 cup peeled and diced mango

1 medium ripe peach, peeled, pitted, and diced

1 cup finely chopped red onion

1 cup peeled and diced cucumber

1 tablespoon balsamic vinegar

1 tablespoon lime juice

1 teaspoon chili powder

½ teaspoon ground cumin

1 tablespoon chopped fresh cilantro

1 tablespoon chopped fresh parsley

½ teaspoon kosher salt

1. In a medium bowl, mix all ingredients together. Chill at least 4 hours before serving.

Per Serving: Calories 41; Fat 0.33g; Sodium 210mg; Carbs 9.74g; Fiber 1.5g; Sugar 7.42g; Protein 0.92g

Italian Seasoning Mix

Prep Time: 15 minutes | Cook Time: 0 minute | Serves: 4

6 tsp. marjoram, dried

6 tsp. thyme leaves, dried

6 tsp. rosemary, dried

6 tsp. savory, ground

3 tsp. sage, dry, ground

6 tsp. oregano leaves, dried

6 tsp. basil leaves, dried

1. Combine all ingredients. 2. Store the leftover mix for future use.

Per Serving: Calories 17; Fat 0.41g; Sodium 2mg; Carbs 3.9g; Fiber 2.5g; Sugar 0.11g; Protein 0.61g

Herbed Oil

½ cup extra-virgin olive oil

1 teaspoon dried basil

1 teaspoon dried parsley

1 teaspoon fresh rosemary leaves

2 teaspoons dried oregano

⅛ teaspoon salt

1. Pour the oil into a small bowl and stir in the basil, rosemary, parsley, oregano, and salt while whisking the oil with a fork. 2. You can make the herbed oil up to 2 days in advance and keep refrigerated.

Per Serving: Calories 241; Fat 27.05g; Sodium 79mg; Carbs 0.53g; Fiber 0.3g; Sugar 0.03g; Protein 0.12g

Conclusion

In conclusion, the 30-Day Whole Foods diet has equipped you with the tools and knowledge to make informed, health-conscious decisions about your food. It has shown you the value of eating whole, unprocessed foods and has likely reshaped your relationship with food in a positive way. As you move forward, let the lessons of this diet inspire you to continue prioritizing your health, making mindful food choices, and enjoying the vibrant benefits of a whole foods lifestyle. Embrace this new way of eating, and continue to explore the endless possibilities that whole foods have to offer.

Appendix 1 Measurement Conversion Chart

VOLUME EQUIVALENTS (LIQUID)

US STANDARD	US STANDARD (OUNCES)	METRIC (APPROXIMATE)
2 tablespoons	1 fl.oz	30 mL
¼ cup	2 fl.oz	60 mL
½ cup	4 fl.oz	120 mL
1 cup	8 fl.oz	240 mL
1½ cup	12 fl.oz	355 mL
2 cups or 1 pint	16 fl.oz	475 mL
4 cups or 1 quart	32 fl.oz	1 L
1 gallon	128 fl.oz	4 L

VOLUME EQUIVALENTS (DRY)

US STANDARD	METRIC (APPROXIMATE)
⅛ teaspoon	0.5 mL
¼ teaspoon	1 mL
½ teaspoon	2 mL
¾ teaspoon	4 mL
1 teaspoon	5 mL
1 tablespoon	15 mL
¼ cup	59 mL
½ cup	118 mL
¾ cup	177 mL
1 cup	235 mL
2 cups	475 mL
3 cups	700 mL
4 cups	1 L

TEMPERATURES EQUIVALENTS

FAHRENHEIT(F)	CELSIUS© (APPROXIMATE)
225 °F	107 °C
250 °F	120 °C
275 °F	135 °C
300 °F	150 °C
325 °F	160 °C
350 °F	180 °C
375 °F	190 °C
400 °F	205 °C
425 °F	220 °C
450 °F	235 °C
475 °F	245 °C
500 °F	260 °C

WEIGHT EQUIVALENTS

US STANDARD	METRIC (APPROXINATE)
1 ounce	28 g
2 ounces	57 g
5 ounces	142 g
10 ounces	284 g
15 ounces	425 g
16 ounces (1 pound)	455 g
1.5pounds	680 g
2pounds	907 g

Appendix 2 Recipes Index

Made in the USA
Las Vegas, NV
16 December 2024

14480721R00062